SRA Reading Mastery

Signature Edition

Storybook 2

Siegfried Engelmann
Elaine C. Bruner

McGraw Hill · SRA

Columbus, OH

SRAonline.com

 SRA

READING MASTERY ® is a registered trademark of The McGraw-Hill Companies, Inc.
Copyright © 2008 by SRA/McGraw-Hill.

Printed in the United States of America.

Send all inquiries to this address:
SRA/McGraw-Hill
4400 Easton Commons
Columbus, OH 43219

ISBN: 978-0-07-612459-6
MHID: 0-07-612459-2

13 14 15 DOW 13 12

The **McGraw·Hill** Companies

Contents

read the Item

If the teacher says "for," say "Of."

don Is a Super man

Who gave don a dime?

Where was the woman with the cape and the cap?

how could don be a super man?

don said, "I hope this works." Then he tapped the dime one time, two times, three times. There was the sound of thunder. "booooooommmmmm."

"What was that?" don asked. he looked at his hand. The dime was still there. Then don saw that he had a cape and a cap. "Wow," don said. "When I tapped that dime, I became a super man."

don said, "I must keep this dime. I will tape it to my arm." and he did. Then he said, "now I will see if I am a super man."

don kicked the wall. "Pow." he made a big hole in the wall. don smiled. "Wow," he said. "I am a super man." he hopped around the store. ⑤

he hit the wall again. "Pow." he made another hole in the wall. now there were two holes in the wall.

don hopped around the hat shop hitting things. he said, "I hate hats."

"Pow." he hit a hat box and made a hole in it. Then he said, "I hate mops." So he broke the mop.

"This is fun," he said. by now the store was a mess. There were holes in the wall. The hats had holes in them. The doors had holes in them.

don said, "no one can stop me now. I am a super man."

To be continued

read the Item

When the teacher says "Saw," say "Was."

don has Super fun

Who gave don the dime?

Where did he tape the dime?

Was he doing good things?

did don mope after he became a super man?

don was hopping around the store in his cap and his cape. he was hitting the walls and making holes. he was having a lot of fun.

all at once he stopped. he said, "I will go outside and show what a super man I am."

When don left the store, he didn't open the door. he ran into the door. "Crash."

Some boys were standing outside the store. They said, "look at that funny man in a cap and a cape."

don said, "I am no funny man. I am

★ a super man."

don ran to a car that was parked near the store. he picked the car up and gave it a big heave. The car crashed into another car.⑤

The boys yelled, "let's get out of here. That man is a nut."

"Come back," don shouted. "let me show you how super I am."

but the boys did not come back. They ran as fast as they could go.

don said, "I think I will fly to the top of this store." So he did. Then he said, "I think I will dive down to the street." So he did. he took a dive. "Crash." he made a big hole in the street.

"This is a lot of fun," don said.

To be continued

read the Item

If the teacher says "Of," say "for."

don makes a mess

The woman who gave don the dime told him that he was to do good. but was don doing good?

don said, "When I worked in the hat store, I would mope and mop. but now I can have fun. I can fly. I can pick up cars and throw them around. I can do anything I want."

don walked down the street. a man said, "look at that funny man in the cap and cape."

That made don mad. he stopped and said, "I have this cape and this cap because I am a super man."

The man said, "You don't look like a super man to me."

don walked over to a bus. he picked up the bus. Then he gave it a heave. "Crash." The bus was bent.

The man said, "let me out of here." and he ran down the street.⑤

"Come back," don shouted, but the man kept on running.

don walked to a school. boys and girls were coming out of the school. don said, "boys and girls, I am a super man."

One girl said, "You look like a nut in that cap and cape."

a boy said, "let's see how fast you can run."

"I will show you," don said.

he ran so fast that the boys and girls could not see him. "Crash." don ran into the school and made a big hole in the side of the school.

One of the boys said, "Stop that. You

are making a mess out of our school. I
don't like you."

"but you must like me," don said. "I
am a super man, and the boys and girls
love super men."

"We hate you," all the boys and girls
said. Then they ran away. don was sad. he
sat down and began to mope.

To be continued

read the Item

If the teacher says "When," say "Then."

don mopes

The woman in the hat store told don to do good. but did don do what the woman said?

don had made holes in walls. he crashed a car and a bus. he ran into the side of a school. The boys and girls began to shout, "We hate you." Then they ran away.

don began to mope. he said, "I am a super man. but nobody likes me." a tear ran down don's cheek. Then another tear ran down his cheek.

all at once don looked down and saw that he did not have his cape. There was no cap on his head.

don said, "I must see if I am still super."

don ran to the street as fast as he could go. but he did not go very fast. he stopped at a parked car and tried to pick it up. he could not do that.⑤

"I am no longer super," he said. "I will tap the dime again." but the tape and the dime were not on his arm.

Slowly, don walked back to the hat store. he was very sad. he said, "The woman who gave me the dime told me to be a good super man. but I did not do good." It was dark inside the store, but don could see the holes in the walls and the holes in the doors and the holes in the hats.

don sat near the mop and began to mope. "I must fix up this store," he said. he began to clean up the mess when a sound came from the stairs.

"Come down here, don," somebody called.

To be continued

read the Item

When the teacher says "hate," say "hat."

don Works Super hard

Somebody called don from the stairs. don went down the stairs. It was dim down there, but don could see the woman who gave him the dime. The woman had a cap and a cape just like don's.

The woman said, "You did not do good. but I think you are sorry. So I will let you try to be a super man again."

"Oh, thank you," don said. "I will try to be good."

The woman held up the dime. She said, "but before I give you the dime back, you must make up for all the bad things you did."

"I will, I will," don said.

don looked at that dime. When he looked up, the woman was not around. don went up the stairs. he said, "I must clean up the mess I made."

So don began to work super hard.⑤ he fixed walls and doors and hats. Then he mopped up. Then he fixed a car and a bus. Then he went back to the school and began to fix the wall.

When he was done with the wall, a truck stopped in front of the school. a little man began to carry big bags from the truck. The bags were bigger than the man. don jumped up and ran over to the man.

"let me help you," don said. "You are too small for this job."

The man said, "This is the only job I can get. my baby is sick and I must work."

"I will help you," don said.

This is almost the end.

read the Item

When the teacher says "here," say "her."

don does good Things

don helped the little man take big bags from the truck. Then don went back to the store. The woman in the cape and cap was standing inside the store. She handed don the dime and said, "I think you will make a good super man."

don took the dime and said, "Thank you."

Then he taped the dime to his arm. Then he began to tap the dime. When he had tapped the dime three times, "boooooommmmmm" came the sound of thunder. don looked down and saw that he had a cape. and there was a cap on his head. "I am super again," don said.

When he was going out the door, he

stopped and said, "I must do something good." he sat down and began to think. Then he said, "I've got it."

he jumped up and began to fly.⑤ he went this way and that way. he was looking for a truck. When he saw it, he dropped down to the street. he ran up to the truck. The little man was in the truck. don said, "get out of that truck."

The little man got out. "What do you want?" he asked don.

don handed the dime to the little man. "here," don said. "You need this dime more than I do." Then don told the man how the dime works. "Tap the dime three times and you will be a super man. but you must be a good super man."

The man tapped the dime. "boooooommmmmm." he became a super man. and he was the best super man there ever was. he did good things. he fixed things. he worked hard. before long his baby got well, and he was very happy. but he wasn't as happy as don was.

don was no longer a super man. but he did not care. he liked his job. he didn't mope. he was happy because he did the most super thing of all. he helped somebody else.

The end

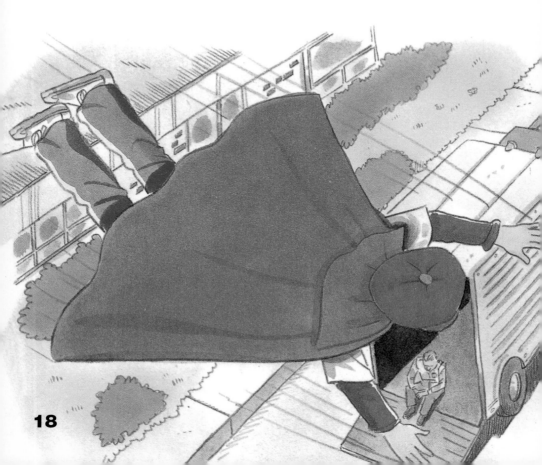

read the Item

When the teacher says "dime," say "dim."

Sid Worked in a Seed Shop

Sid had a job. he worked in a seed shop. That shop had lots of little plants.

The boss of the shop had a bad leg. So she walked with a cane. When she was not walking with her cane, she left her cane in a big can near the door.

One day the boss said, "I must hop in the truck and go to the other side of town. You stay here and take care of the shop."

So the boss got her cane from the can and went to the truck. When she got in her truck, she said, "There is a pile of notes on the table. Take care of them."★

after the boss left, Sid went to the table and began to read those notes. here is

what one note said. "Send ten pine trees."
but Sid did not read those words.⑤ here is
what he said, "Send ten pin trees."

Then he looked around the shop for
pins. he stuck the pins in sticks. he made
ten little trees of pins. Then he said, "I
don't know what anybody wants with pin
trees, but I will send them out."

and he did.

Then he picked up the next note. It
said, "fix the window pane." but here is
what Sid said when he looked at the words.
"fix the window pan."

Sid looked around the shop for a
window pan. he said, "I can't see a window
pan, so I will make one." and he did. he
made a big tin pan. he nailed it over the
window. Then he said to himself, "I am
doing a fine job."

more to come

Send ten pine trees.

read the Item

When the teacher says "her," say "here."

Sid Sends a Con to the farm

Sid did not read well. One note told him to send pine trees. but Sid sent pin trees. another note told him to fix the window pane. but Sid made a window pan.

now Sid went back to the table and picked up another note. The note said, "Tape the oak tree near the door." but Sid did not read the words on the note. here is what Sid said, "Tap the oak tree near the door."

he said, "That seems like a funny thing to do. but I will do it." So Sid went to the oak tree near the door. he tapped it with his hand. Then he went back to the table to read more notes.

here is what the next note said, "Send

a cone to Sam's tree farm."

but here is what Sid said when he looked at the words, "Send a con to Sam's tree farm."⑤

Sid said to himself, "We don't have cons in this shop. Cons are in jail." So Sid called the jail and said to the jailer, "do you have a con that you can send to a tree farm?"

The jailer said, "Yes, we have a fine con. he is getting out of jail today. he needs a job. I will be glad to send him to a tree farm."

"good," Sid said. "Send the con to Sam's tree farm."

after Sid took care of the con, he said to himself, "I am really doing a good job. The boss will be proud of me."

do you think the boss will be proud of the things that Sid has done?

more to come

Tape the oak tree near the door.

Read the Item

When the teacher says "Tap," say "Tape."

Sid Plants Seeds in Slop

Sid was reading notes that were on the table. But he was not reading these notes the right way. A note told him to send a cone to a tree farm. But Sid sent a con to the tree farm. Before that he tapped the oak tree near the door. But the note did not tell him to tap the tree. It told him to tape that tree.

Now Sid went back to the pile of notes on the table. He picked up a note that said, "Plant seeds on the slope." There was a slope in back of the shop. That is where the boss planted a lot of little plants. But Sid did not read the note the right way. Here is what Sid said, "Plant seeds in the slop."

Then he said, "These notes are very funny. But I will do what they say."⑤ So Sid grabbed some seeds and went outside. "Where is the slop?" he asked. He looked here and there. Then he saw a big pile of mud near the road. He said, "That must be the slop." So Sid dumped seeds in the mud.

When he was near the side of the shop, a truck stopped in back of the shop. The boss got out of the truck. She was walking with her cane. The boss said, "What are you doing out here?"

Sid said, "I just planted seeds in the slop."

The boss looked at Sid. Then the boss asked, "What did you do?"

Sid told her. The boss got mad. "Not in the slop," the boss yelled. "On the slope. Plant the seeds on the slope."

Sid felt very sad.

More to come

Read the Item

When the teacher says "Cone," say "Con."

The Boss Gets Mad

Sid was sad and the boss was mad. The boss yelled at Sid for planting seeds in the slop. When the boss was tired of yelling, she said, "Let's go to the shop and see how well you did the other things the notes told you to do."

So Sid and the boss went to the shop. The boss dropped her cane into the can. She went to the table and picked up a note. Then she said, "Did you send out ten pine trees?"

"Pine trees?" Sid asked. "I sent out pin trees."

That made the boss mad. She walked around the room. Then she said, "I hope that you did a better job with the other notes."

She picked up another note. Then she said, "Did you fix the window pane?"

"Window pane?" Sid asked. "I made a window pan." ⑤

The boss got her cane from the can. She walked around the room. She yelled and yelled. Then she said, "I hope you sent a cone to Sam's tree farm."

"No," Sid said. "I sent a con from the jail."

The boss sat down on the floor. "This is a fine mess," she said. Then she asked, "Did you tape the oak tree?"

"No," Sid said. "I tapped the oak tree." Sid was very, very sad. He wanted to do a good job, but he didn't read what the notes said.

More to come

Read the Item

If the teacher says "Pin," say "Pine."

The Boss Teaches Sid to Read

Sid felt so sad that a tear ran down his cheek. The boss was so mad that she was sitting on the floor, tapping her cane and looking at Sid. The boss said, "You didn't plant seeds on the slope. You planted seeds in the slop."

"Yes," Sid said. "I didn't mean to do a bad job. But I don't read very well."

The boss said, "Well, I will teach you how to read. If you are going to help me in this shop, you must be good at reading."

So the boss began to teach Sid how to read words like **pane** and **rode** and **tape** and **time**. Sid sat at the side of the boss and the boss made notes for Sid to read. At first, Sid did not read the words like **hope** and **rob**. But every day, Sid would read a little better.⑤ And before a week went by, Sid could read the words very well. The boss made up some hard notes. One note said, "Hide a bit of cheese near the mop." Another note said, "Tape a cap to my cape." But the boss could not fool Sid.

Now, when the boss leaves the shop, she says, "Sid, read the notes on the table and do what the notes tell you to do." That's what Sid does. If a note tells him to fix a window pane, he does it. If a note tells him to send a cone to a tree farm, he sends a cone, not a con. Sid is very happy and so is the boss.

The end

hop hope
rop rope

Dan the Teacher

A girl named Ann had a dog. The dog was named Dan. One day Dan went to school with Ann.

The teacher said, "Ann, take that dog out of this school. Schools are for boys and girls. Schools are not for dogs."

Ann said, "But this dog is very smart. He likes to read and he likes to add."

The teacher said, "I will let that dog stay, but if he makes a sound, I will make him leave."

So the dog sat down to read a book to himself. The boys and girls worked with the teacher.

But then the teacher was called out of the room.

One boy said, "We do not have a teacher ★ now."

Dan walked up and said, "I will be your teacher."

So he began to teach. He was one of the best teachers the boys and girls had ever seen.⑤ He helped the children read a very hard book. And he helped them spell hard words.

At the end of the day, some of the children went up to the dog and gave him a big kiss. They said, "We hope that Dan will be our teacher from now on."

More to come

Dan, the Teacher's Helper

Dan was a dog that liked to read and liked to add. He went to school with a girl named Ann. When the teacher left the room, Dan became the teacher. He did a fine job.

The next day Dan came to school. He sat in the back of the room and began to read his book. The teacher began to do work with the boys and girls. But some of the boys and girls said, "We want Dan to be our teacher."

That made the teacher sad. She said, "I cannot let Dan be the teacher."

The boys and girls said, "Oh, that's too bad. He is a fine teacher."

The teacher said, "But I can let Dan be a teacher's helper. Dan can help you with your seat work."

The boys and girls smiled. Dan wagged

his tail. He felt proud. Ann also felt very proud.⑤

So now the boys and girls in Ann's room come to school very early. They say that they have the best room in town. They have a very smart teacher and that teacher has a fine helper. Do you think that the boys and girls in this room are lucky?

This is the end.

The Tame Tiger Who Liked Ice Cream

There once was a tame tiger. This tiger did not bite children. He didn't eat goats or sheep. He said, "I like ice cream. So I will go to town and get some."

But the tiger didn't have any cash. He said, "I will fill my pouch with round stones. I hope that the man at the ice cream store likes round stones."

So the tiger filled his pouch with round stones. Then he walked to town. He went up to the man at the ice cream stand.

"I don't have any cash," the tiger said. "But I have a pouch filled with pretty round stones."

"Let's see them," the man said.

So the tiger showed the man his stones. The man said, "I like those stones. They are pretty."

The tiger gave the pouch to the man.⑤

Then the tiger said, "I want a big cone, and I want some string."

The man said, "What will you do with a big cone and some string?"

"Wait and see," the tiger said.

What do you think the tiger did? He ate the ice cream from the cone. Then he put the big cone on his head with a string.

The tiger said, "I love ice cream and I love hats. I ate the ice cream and now I have the best hat in town."

The man at the ice cream stand said, "That tiger is very tame. He is also very smart."

The end

40

Spot Meets a Tall Girl

One day Spot went for a walk. Soon she met a tall girl. The girl said, "How are you?"

Spot did not hear that girl. She said to herself, "That girl wants to know who I am."

So Spot said, "They call me Spot."

The tall girl shook her head. Then she shouted, "How are you?"

"I'm fine," Spot shouted back.

Then the tall girl began to walk away. Spot asked the question, "Where are you going?"

"I am going to the mall in town," she answered.

Spot said to herself, "That girl said that she will fall."

Spot ran over to the girl. "Sit down," she said. "Then you won't fall down."

The girl smiled. Then she yelled, "I'm not going to fall. I'm going to the mall."

"Oh," Spot said. "You're going to the mall." Then Spot asked the question, "Can I go with you?" ⑤

"Yes," the tall girl said. "Come to the mall and we will have a ball."

So Spot and the girl started to walk to the mall.

Soon they met a fat pig. That pig was crying. The girl went over to the pig and asked, "Why are you crying?"

The pig told her why he was crying. You will find out why when you read the next story.

More next time

43

Spot Gets a Wig

Spot and the tall girl were on their way to the mall when they met a fat pig. That pig was crying. The tall girl asked the pig why he was crying. And the pig answered, "Because I cannot find my wig. I had a big red wig. A big wind came up and took the wig with it."

The girl said, "Well, come to the mall with us and I'll get you another wig."

So Spot and the girl and the fat pig went to the mall. The girl stopped in front of a wig shop. She said to the pig, "Look in that shop and see which wig you want."

The fat pig looked and looked. Then he said, "I want that big yellow wig. That wig will make me look pretty."

"You wait here," the girl said. She went into the wig shop.⑤ Soon she came out of the shop with a big yellow wig. She gave it to the pig. He was very happy. He said, "I love this wig."

But then what do you think happened? Spot began to cry. The tall girl asked, "Why are you crying, Spot?"

"I don't have a pretty wig," she answered. "I want one too."

The girl shook her head. "Wait here," the girl said. When she came out of the shop, she was holding another yellow wig. She gave it to Spot.

Spot said, "Now I am pretty too."

Do you think she looked very pretty in that big yellow wig?

This story is over.

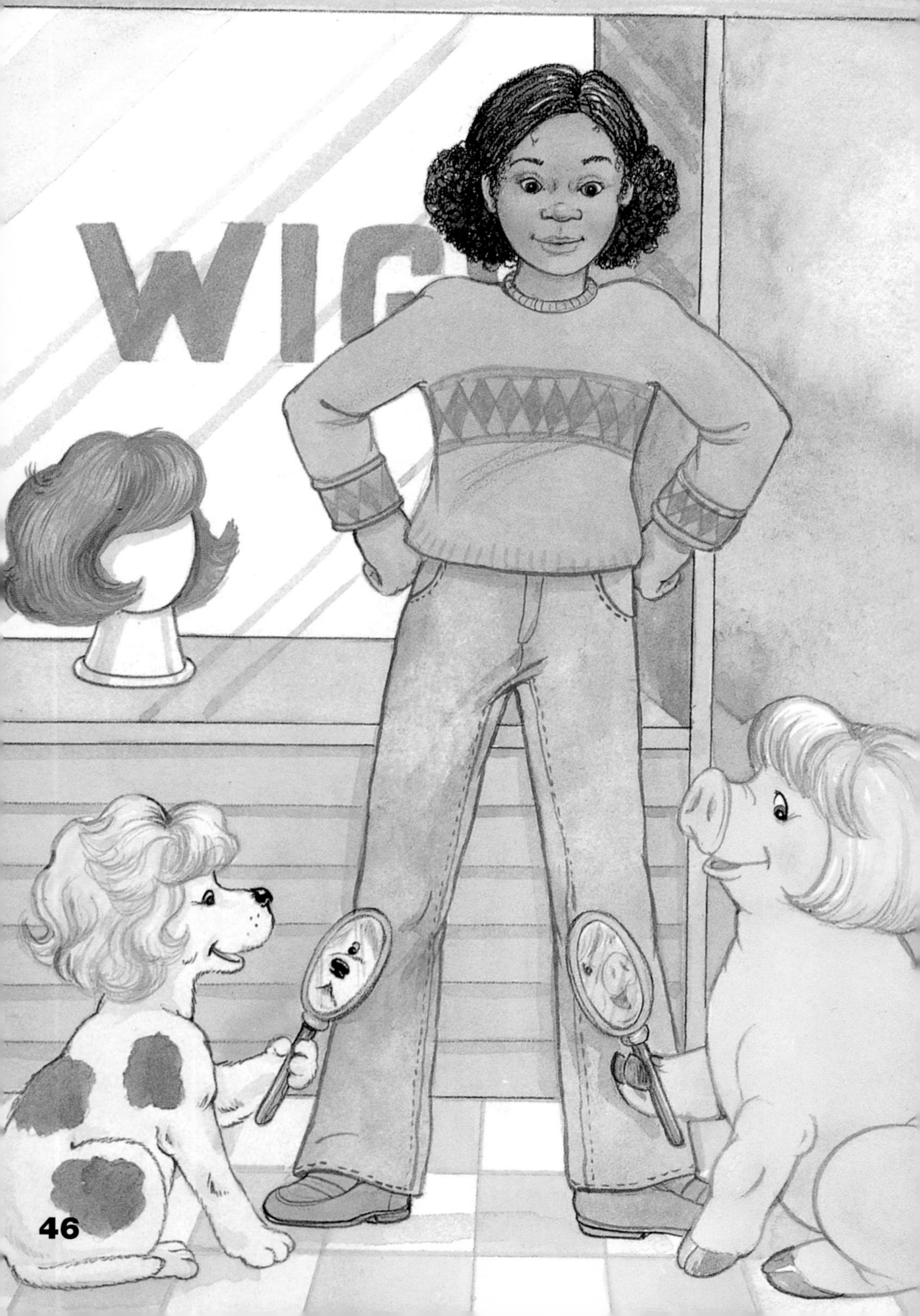
WIG

The Ugly Duckling

There once was a mother duck who found a big egg. She said, "I will put this egg with my other eggs." And so she did.

Soon all of the eggs hatched. The little eggs hatched and the big egg that she found hatched. What do you think came out of the big egg? A funny-looking duckling. He was big, and he kept falling down when he tried to walk.

The other ducklings called him names. "You are ugly," they said. "You are an ugly duckling."

The ugly duckling was sad. None of the other ducklings would play with him. They just called him names. "Boy, are you ever an ugly duckling," they would say.

The ★ ugly duckling said to himself, "I am so ugly and nobody likes me."

The ducklings grew up. The little

ducklings grew up to be pretty ducks, just like their mother and father.⑤ And what do you think happened to the big ugly duckling?

One day all of the ducklings saw a pretty swan swimming on the pond. They all stopped and looked at the swan. "My, my," they said. "That swan is so pretty."

They swam over to the swan and said, "Hello, pretty swan." And the swan said, "Hello."

Then one of the ducks said, "That is the ugly duckling." And it was. The ugly duckling was not a duckling at all. He had grown up to be a pretty swan.

So the swan and the ducks became good pals. And the ducks never called the swan ugly again.

This story is over.

The Kitten Needs a Home

A little kitten was sad because she did not have a home. She said, "I must find a home."

She looked in a mail box. She said, "This will be my home." And she went into the mail box.

It was very dark in that mail box. The little kitten said, "I do not want to live in this mail box because it is too dark."

Then she looked at a nest in a tree. She said, "This will be my home." She went up the tree and sat in the nest.

Then it started to snow.

The kitten said, "I do not want to live in this nest because it is too cold." She said, "I must find another home."

She began to walk from the nest. Then she saw a fish bowl. She said, "This will be my home."⑤ She went into the fish bowl, but she got wet. She said, "I do not want to live in this fish bowl because I get too wet."

She started to cry. Just then a little girl came by. The girl asked, "Why are you crying?"

The kitten answered, "Because I do not have a home."

More to come

The Kitten's New Home

A kitten was sad because she did not have a home. She tried to live in a mail box and a nest and a fish bowl. But she did not like these homes.

She started to cry. A small girl asked her, "Why are you crying?"

The kitten told the small girl about the mail box and the nest and the fish bowl. Then the kitten said, "I am sad because I have no home."

The girl said, "I live on a farm. We have a big farm house. We have a barn. And it is fun to play in the barn. We have sheep and cows. And the cows give lots of milk. We have everything but one thing."

"What is that?" the kitten asked.

The girl said, "We don't have a kitten and I love kittens."

Then the small girl said, "Would you like to live on our farm?" ⑤

The kitten jumped into the girl's arms. "I will be your kitten," the kitten said. She gave the girl one kiss and then another kiss.

So the girl and the kitten went to the farm. The kitten had a home and the girl had a kitten. She loved that kitten.

This story is over.

Boo the Ghost

There was a big old house near the town. Six ghosts lived in that old house. And five of those ghosts were very mean. They liked to play tricks on boys and girls. They liked to scare people.

Every night after the sun went down, those five ghosts would say, "What can we do that is mean?" The five ghosts would name some mean things.

Then the five ghosts would go out to do mean things. Sometimes they would hide on a dark street. When a child walked by, they would jump out and say, "Oooooow." The child would run and they would say, "Ho, ho."

Sometimes they would go to a farm and make the horses so scared that the horses would run from the barn. The farmer would come out to see what had happened. The ghosts would hide.⑤ When he was near the barn, they would all jump at him and say, "Ooooooow." And the farmer would run back into his house.

Five ghosts were mean. But the other ghost who lived in the old house was not mean. His name was Boo. He didn't like to scare horses. Boo liked to ride on horses. He didn't like to scare small boys and girls. He liked to play games with them. He didn't like to do mean things. He liked to do things that made everybody happy.

But the people in town were afraid of him. Farmers were also afraid of him. Boys and girls were also afraid. But the ghosts that he lived with were not afraid of him. They didn't like him. They said, "You are not a good ghost because you are not mean."

More to come

Boo Leaves the House

Boo was a ghost, but he was not mean like the other ghosts that lived with him. Those five ghosts were very mean and they liked to do mean things. But Boo was not mean. While the other ghosts went out to do mean things, he would read.

Then one night, the other five ghosts made Boo leave the old house. They came back from playing mean tricks. Boo was sitting in his seat reading a book. The other ghosts said, "You are not a good ghost, so you must leave this house."

"Where will I go?" Boo asked.

"We don't care where you go," the biggest ghost said. "Just get out of this house."

So Boo picked up his heap of books and left the old house. As he walked from the house, he could hear the other ghosts talking and laughing. They were planning to do mean things. ⑤

Boo walked down the road. When he was near the town, he stopped. "I hear somebody crying."

Boo looked around in the dark. At last he came to a stream and saw who was crying. It was a big green frog. The frog looked at Boo and stopped crying. The frog said, "Are you really a ghost?"

"Yes," Boo said. "And are you really a talking frog?"

"No," the frog said. "I am a king, but a monster cast a spell over me and turned me into a frog. I am very sad."

"Can I help you?" Boo asked.

"No," the frog said. "Nobody can help me now."

More to come

Boo Goes to the Castle

The five mean ghosts had made Boo
leave the old house. When Boo was walking
to town, he found a talking frog. The frog
was near a stream. But the frog was not
really a frog. It was a king. A monster had
cast a spell on the king and turned him
into a frog.

"I will help you," Boo said. "Just tell
me where the monster stays."

The frog said, "The monster is in my
castle. That castle is on the other side of
town."

"You wait here," Boo said. "I will be
back."

Boo floated up into the sky. He floated
over the town like a bird. Soon he came to
the castle ★ on the other side of town.
When he floated near the castle, the
hounds began to howl. Boo floated to the

top of the wall that went around the castle.⑤ The hounds were howling and howling.

Then the door to the castle opened and out came the meanest-looking monster Boo had ever seen. That monster roared, "Who is out here? Who is making my hounds howl?"

Boo did not say a thing. He just watched the monster.

The monster roared, "If you don't leave, I'll get you. I'll turn you into a frog or a toad."

When the monster went back into the castle, Boo floated from the wall. He found a window and went inside the castle. He could see the monster. Boo said to himself, "That monster is really mean."

The monster was holding a gold rod. She was saying, "As long as I have this

magic rod, I can cast a spell over anybody.
I can turn anybody into a frog or a toad."

Boo said to himself, "I must get that
magic rod from the monster."

Stop

Boo Gets a Fish Tail

Boo was inside the monster's castle.
The monster had a magic rod that was
made of gold. The monster was saying that
she could cast spells on people as long as
she had the magic rod.

Boo said to himself, "I must get that
rod from the monster."

Boo said, "I will try to scare the
monster." So Boo made himself as big and
as mean as he could. But he was still
pretty small and he didn't really look
mean.

He floated down at the monster.
"Oooooow," he said.

The monster laughed. "What's this?"
she said. "A little ghost thinks he can fill
me with fear. I'll show him some fear."

The monster held up the magic rod.
"Bod bode, bed bead," she said. All at once,
Boo felt funny. He looked down and saw

that he had the tail of a fish.⑤ He had a big fin growing from his back.

"That should hold you for a while," the monster said, and she began to laugh. "Now get out of here before I turn you into a leaf."

Boo really got out of there, because he was really scared. When he was far from the castle, he stopped and looked at himself. He was part fish and part ghost. He wanted to cry. But he didn't cry.

He said to himself, "I must think of some way to get that gold rod from the monster. If I get the rod, I could turn myself back into a real ghost. But that gold rod is my only hope."

Boo sat and began to think. He needed a plan. He sat for a long time. Then all at once, he said, "I have a plan now. And I think it will work."

Stop

Boo's Plan Works

Boo had a plan for getting the gold rod from the monster. Boo floated back to the old house where the other ghosts stayed. He floated inside the house. The other five ghosts were eating their big meal. They always ate a big meal before they went out to do mean things.

When the ghosts saw Boo, they stopped eating and said, "What are you doing here? We made you leave this house. So get out."

Boo said, "I am here because I have found somebody you can't scare."

The five ghosts jumped up from the table. The biggest ghost made himself as big as a horse. Then he made himself look meaner than the monster. "I can scare anybody," he shouted.

The other ghosts made themselves look big and mean, too. "We can scare anybody," they said.

"No, you can't," Boo said.⑤ "There is a monster near here who is so mean that you can't scare her. And she can do magic things. Look at what she did to me."

The five ghosts looked at Boo's fish tail and his fin. They started to laugh.

"That monster can play magic tricks on you," the biggest ghost said. "But you are not much of a ghost. Her magic won't work on us. We are real ghosts."

"No," Boo said. "She will turn you into a log or into a frog.

"Come on," one of the ghosts said. "Let's go get that monster. Let's see her try to play tricks on us."

The other ghosts said, "Yes, let's go. Lead us to her."

Had Boo's plan worked?

Stop

The Ghosts Meet the Monster

Boo was leading the way to the monster's castle. The biggest ghost said, "I'll scare her so much she'll turn into a mouse." Another ghost said, "I'll scare her so much she'll turn into a bug."

Soon, Boo and the other ghosts came to the castle. The hounds began to howl. One of the ghosts floated down near the hounds. He made himself as big as a horse. Then he said, "Eeeeeeeeeee." The hounds ran away like a flash.

Then the ghosts floated into the castle. The monster was sitting at one end of a long table. The gold rod was at the other end. One of the ghosts rammed into the table and broke the table into a thousand bits. Another ghost picked up the monster's plate and heaved it at the monster. "Plop." It hit her in the nose.

Another ghost got behind the monster and made a loud sound.⑤ "Rrrrr." When the monster turned around, the biggest ghost flew at the monster and knocked her down. All of the ghosts were howling and making themselves look as mean as they could.

The monster got up. "What's going on here?" she shouted.

Then all five ghosts flew at her.

"I'm leaving," the monster said. And she ran away from the castle as fast as she could go.

The biggest ghost flew over and grabbed the gold rod.

"This must be a magic rod," he said. "We can have a lot of fun with this rod. We can turn Boo into a leaf."

"That's a fine plan," the other ghosts said.

Stop

The Ghosts Turn on Boo

The biggest ghost had the magic rod. He was going to turn Boo into a leaf. He held the rod and said, "Turn Boo into a leaf." But nothing happened.

"This thing doesn't work," the biggest ghost said.

Another ghost looked at the rod and said, "You're not saying the right words. You have to say funny words if you want to cast a spell. Say something funny."

The biggest ghost said, "Bine bin, fine fin." Nothing happened to Boo. But the biggest ghost turned into a big red flower. The other ghosts laughed. "That was a good trick," they said.

One of the other ghosts grabbed the rod. He said, "I never did like that big ghost anyhow. Now I'm the biggest ghost and I will make this magic rod work for me."

He held the rod and said, "Tim time, cop cope." ⑤ Nothing happened to Boo, but the ghost who was holding the rod turned into a leaf.

The other mean ghosts laughed and laughed. Then one of them picked up the rod and said, "Now I am the biggest ghost. And I will find a way to make that rod work."

He held the rod and looked at it for a long time. Then he said, "I see words on the side of this rod. Those words tell how to cast spells."

The other mean ghosts said, "Well, read the words."

The ghost who was holding the rod said, "I can't read."

Stop

Boo Casts Some Spells

The ghosts had found words on the side of the rod. The ghost who was holding the rod said, "I can't read." Then he looked at the other mean ghosts. "Who can read these words?" he asked.

"Not me," they all said. Then the three ghosts looked at Boo.

"You can read," one ghost said. "So read these words and tell us how to turn you into a leaf."

Boo said, "Hand me the rod and I will do the best I can."

So the ghost handed the rod to Boo, and Boo looked at the words on the rod. Then Boo held the rod and said, "Bit bite, ben bean."

Nothing happened to Boo, but the other ghosts began to smile. One ghost said, "I don't feel mean anymore."

Another ghost said, "I feel ★ like playing games with the boys and girls in town." ⑤

Another ghost said, "Not me. I feel like going out and helping a farmer milk cows."

Before they left, they turned to Boo and said, "Thank you for making us feel so good."

After they left, Boo held up the rod and said, "Sip dim, dime dup." The flower turned back into a smiling ghost. And the leaf turned back into a smiling ghost. They both gave Boo a kiss and they left for school.

"We want to read books," they said.

Boo said some magic words to make his fins and tail go away. Then he said, "Now I will go find the frog and turn him back into a king."

More to come

Everybody Is Happy

Boo had turned the mean ghosts into smiling ghosts. Then Boo had made his tail and fins go away. Now Boo was on his way to turn the frog back into a king.

Boo found the frog on a log in the stream. Boo held up the magic rod. "Come to the shore," Boo said, "and I will turn you into a king."

"Hot dog," the frog said. He jumped from the log and swam to shore in a flash.

Then Boo said, "Hog, sog, bumpy log," and the frog turned into a king. The king said, "Hot dog, I'm a king again. Hot dog."

The king ran around, and yelled, and shouted, and laughed, and rolled around in the sand. When the king was tired out, Boo told him how the ghosts had scared the monster into leaving the castle.⑤

Then the king said, "Boo, you must
come and live with me in the castle."

"No, no," Boo said, "I couldn't do that."

"Why not?" the king asked.

Boo said, "I, well . . . I, well . . . ." Boo
was shy.

The king said, "You must come and
live with me. As king of this land, I'm
telling you to come and live with me in my
fine castle."

So Boo went to live with the king. And
he lived with the king for years and years
and years.

Things were very good in the land. The
people had a good king. The king had a
good friend. And all of the ghosts in the
land were very good ghosts. The people
didn't say, "Let's not go out at night." They

said, "Let's go out at night. Maybe we can find a ghost and play games with him. Ghosts are fun."

The end

Ott Is in Genie School

Ott was going to school. He was trying to be a genie, but he did not know many genie tricks.

Genies live in bottles. When somebody rubs the bottle, the genie comes out in a puff of smoke. Then the genie says, "Yes, master, what can I do for you?"

The master tells what he wants, and the genie gets him what he wants. If the master wishes for an elephant, the genie makes an elephant appear. If the master wishes for a bag of gold, the genie makes a bag of gold appear.

But Ott could not do these tricks. That is why he was still going to school. And he was not the best of those who were in school. When their teacher told the genies to make an apple appear on the table, Ott made an alligator appear on the table.⑤ When the teacher told Ott to make gold appear on the floor, Ott made a pot of beans appear on the floor.

Then one day, something strange happened. Ott and the other genies were working at getting into a little bottle. All at once, an old woman ran into the school and ran up to the teacher. The old woman said, "We need more genies. Somebody has found an old yellow bottle that should have a genie in it. But we have not had a genie in that bottle for years and years."

"What about all of our other genies?" the teacher asked. "Why can't we send one of them to the yellow bottle?"

"They are all working," the old woman said. "This is a big year for genies. People have been finding old genie bottles all year. Every one of our genies is working, so we will have to send one of the children from your school to the yellow bottle."

More to come

83

Ott Takes a Test

Ott was going to genie school. One day an old woman came in and told Ott's teacher, "We need more genies. We must send one of the children from your school to the yellow bottle."

"No, no," the teacher said. "These children cannot go to work as genies. They are not that smart."

The old woman said, "We cannot wait. The girl who found the yellow bottle may rub it any time, and when she rubs it, a genie must come out of that bottle."

The teacher looked at the children who were working to be genies. The teacher said, "I don't know which of these children to pick. None of them would be a good genie."

The old woman said, "I will give the children a test. The child who does the best on the test will go and work in the yellow bottle."⑤

The old woman walked over to the children. "Here is what I want you to do. Make a peach appear on the floor."

All of the children began to say things to themselves. Then peaches began to appear on the floor—one peach, two peaches, three peaches, and then . . . all of the peaches disappeared under a pile of sand. Ott didn't make a peach appear. He made a beach appear.

"Who did that?" the old woman shouted.

Ott didn't say anything because he didn't know that he had made the beach appear.

The old woman said, "We can't wait anymore. I'll just have to pick one of the children." She looked at each of the children. She stopped in front of Ott.

"You," she said to Ott. "You go to the yellow bottle. Do it now."

Ott smiled and made himself disappear in a puff of smoke. He could not hear his teacher yelling, "No, no, not that one. He never does anything the right way."

More next time

Ott Comes Out of the Bottle

Ott was very happy. He was picked to go into the yellow bottle. It was dark inside that bottle, but Ott didn't care. He was waiting for the girl to rub the bottle. That girl's name was Carla. She had found the bottle in a pile of junk. When she found it, she said, "I like that bottle. I will take it home with me."

So now she was on her way home. She was going down Bide Street. She wasn't thinking about what she was doing.

A bunch of bad boys were always hanging around on Bide Street. Suddenly, Carla saw that three mean boys were following her. One of them said, "What do you have in that bottle?"

"Nothing," Carla said, and she kept on walking.

One of the boys said to the other boys, "Let's take that bottle and bust it."⑤

The boys all went, "Ho, ho, ho."

Carla stopped and looked at the boys. "You better leave me alone," she said. "Or I'll rub this bottle and a genie will come out and beat you up."

"Ho, ho," the boys said. "That girl can really tell lies. Do you think you can fool us with that silly story about the genie?"

Carla didn't know what to do. She didn't really think that there was a genie in the bottle, but she wanted to scare the mean boys. "If you take one more step, I'll rub the bottle."

"I'm going to take that bottle and smash it," one of the boys said. He reached for the bottle. Carla rubbed the bottle. There was a puff of smoke. The boys stopped. They watched as the smoke became a genie.

More to come

Ott Tells Lies

When the mean boys tried to take the bottle from Carla, she rubbed the bottle and Ott appeared.

Ott said, "Oh, master Carla, what can I do for you?"

Carla said, "Give those boys a spanking."

"Yes, master," Ott said. He sounded smart, but he didn't know how to give the boys a spanking. He could only remember the word banking.

"Well," Carla said at last, "are you going to give them a spanking?"

"Yes," Ott said. "A spanking it will be."

Ott waved his hands. Suddenly, Carla, Ott, and the three boys were in a bank. They were banking.

Carla said, "What kind of a genie are you?"

The boys said, "Let's get out of here," and they began to run from the bank as fast as they could go.

Ott was very sad. He said, ★ "Carla, I am a very old genie.⑤ I have been in the bottle for thousands of years. I have not done tricks for thousands of years."

Ott was telling some big lies. He was not a very old genie. He had not lived in the bottle for thousands of years, and he didn't forget how to do genie tricks. He never was able to do them.

Carla said, "Well, can you get us out of this bank and take us home?"

"Yes, master Carla," Ott said. "That should be easy."

Ott folded his arms. He said some words. Boop.

Suddenly, Ott and Carla were standing in the middle of a big city. Carla looked around. Then she said, "This is not home.

This is Rome. Rome is thousands of miles from my home."

More next time

Ott Is a Very Sad Genie

Carla had told Ott to take her home, but Ott didn't take Carla home. He took her to Rome. Carla was getting mad. She was also getting a little scared. She said, "Please get us home this time."

"I will do my best trick," Ott said. He began to spin around. As he was spinning, he said things to himself. Poof. Suddenly, Carla and Ott were standing in the middle of a forest. Carla said, "You must be the poorest genie there is. Where are we now?"

"I don't know," Ott said. "I will have to read my trick book to see what I did to bring us here."

So Ott began to read his trick book and Carla waited and waited. At last, she said, "Could you bring me something to eat while I'm waiting?"

"Yes," Ott said. "What do you want?" ⑤

Carla said, "I would like an apple or a peach."

"An apple and a peach you will have," Ott said. He said some words and what do you think appeared for an apple? An alligator. And what do you think appeared for a peach? A beach.

Carla said, "You are a mess of a genie. I asked for an apple or a peach. All I see is an alligator and a pile of sand."

"I will try again," Ott said. "This time, I will try to get you a hot dog."

Ott said some words to himself. Suddenly, a log appeared. The log was on fire. Carla began to laugh.

"That is not a hot dog," she said. "That's a hot log."

Ott was not laughing. He was very sad. He was very poor at being a genie.

More about Ott and Carla next time

Carla and Ott Can't Get Home

Ott and Carla were in a forest. When Ott tried to get a hot dog for Carla, a hot log appeared. Carla laughed, but Ott felt very sad. Carla said, "Can you call for help? If someone hears us, they can tell us which way to go."

"Yes," Ott said. "I will make a sound that is very loud—very loud." Ott said some words to himself. But there was no loud sound. There was a cloud. Again Carla laughed.

She said, "You tried to make something that was loud, but you made a cloud. So why don't you try to make a cloud? Maybe then you'll make a sound that is loud."

"Yes, master," Ott said. He folded his arms and said some words. Suddenly a loud sound filled the air. "Help, help."

Ott said, "It worked. When I tried to

make the cloud, I made a sound that is loud." ⑤

Then Ott jumped up and down. He shouted and laughed. Then he said, "I've got it. I've got it. I know how to get us home."

"How?" Carla asked. "How?"

"Well," Ott said, still hopping up and down a bit. "When I wished us to go home, we went to Rome. So if I wish us to go to Rome . . . ."

"We will go home," Carla said. She ran over and gave Ott a kiss.

Ott blushed. Then he folded his arms and said some words. Suddenly, Carla seemed to be flying in the air. And then she stopped and looked around.

"Oh nuts," she said. "We're not at home. We are back in Rome."

Ott said, "I don't know how I do that."

More of this story next time

Ott Disappears

Carla was sad. She felt a tear streaming down her cheek. She said, "You are not a very funny genie. Can't you see that I want to go home? I don't want to stay in forests and get logs that are on fire. I don't want to be standing in the middle of Rome. I just want to go home. Do you hear me?"

Ott said, "I'm really very sorry, master." Now a tear was streaming down Ott's cheek. "I must tell you something," he said. "I told you a lie. I am not a very old genie. I have not been resting in that bottle for thousands of years. I am not old and wise. I am still going to genie school."

Carla said, "Well, isn't there some way to get out of this mess? Can you call for help?"

"Yes," Ott said. "That is one of the things I can do."⑤

Ott folded his arms and said some things to himself. Then Carla could see something flying across the sky. Suddenly it began to dive down to Ott. It came closer and closer. Now Carla could see that it was a big, wet fish. Splat. It hit Ott in the face.

Carla said, "You can't even call for help. You're not much help as a genie at all. In fact, I wish you would get out of here."

"Yes, master," Ott said with a tear running down his cheek. Slowly a puff of smoke formed, and slowly Ott disappeared into the smoke. Then the smoke began to flow into the yellow bottle.

Carla picked up the bottle and tossed it as hard as she could. Crash. It went through the window of a house.

More to come

Ott Helps Carla

Carla picked up the bottle and tossed it through the window of a house. Then a big woman came out, holding the bottle. "Who tossed this bottle through my window?" she screamed.

She ran over and grabbed Carla. "You did it, didn't you? You are the one who tossed that bottle through my window."

"Yes, I did," Carla said. "But I didn't mean to. I didn't . . . ."

"I'll show you," the woman said. She put the bottle down. Then she picked up a broom. She was going to spank Carla with the broom.

Carla bent over and rubbed the bottle. Poof. Ott was back.

He said, "I will try to get you out of this, master." Ott said some words. Suddenly the pane of glass in the window was not broken.

"Stop," Carla said. "Look at your window. It is no longer broken."

The woman looked at her window.⑤ "I don't believe it," she said to herself. "I saw the glass go flying this way and that way. Now the glass is back in the window."

The woman dropped the broom and went back into her house. After she left, Carla gave Ott a big hug. "You did it," she said. "You wanted the window to have a pane of glass and you made it happen."

Ott smiled. "I think I'm getting better at being a genie."

Carla said, "Maybe you can get us out of here now."

"I will try very hard," Ott said. "And please, master, don't hate me if I don't do well."

Carla looked at Ott and smiled. "Okay," she said.

More to come

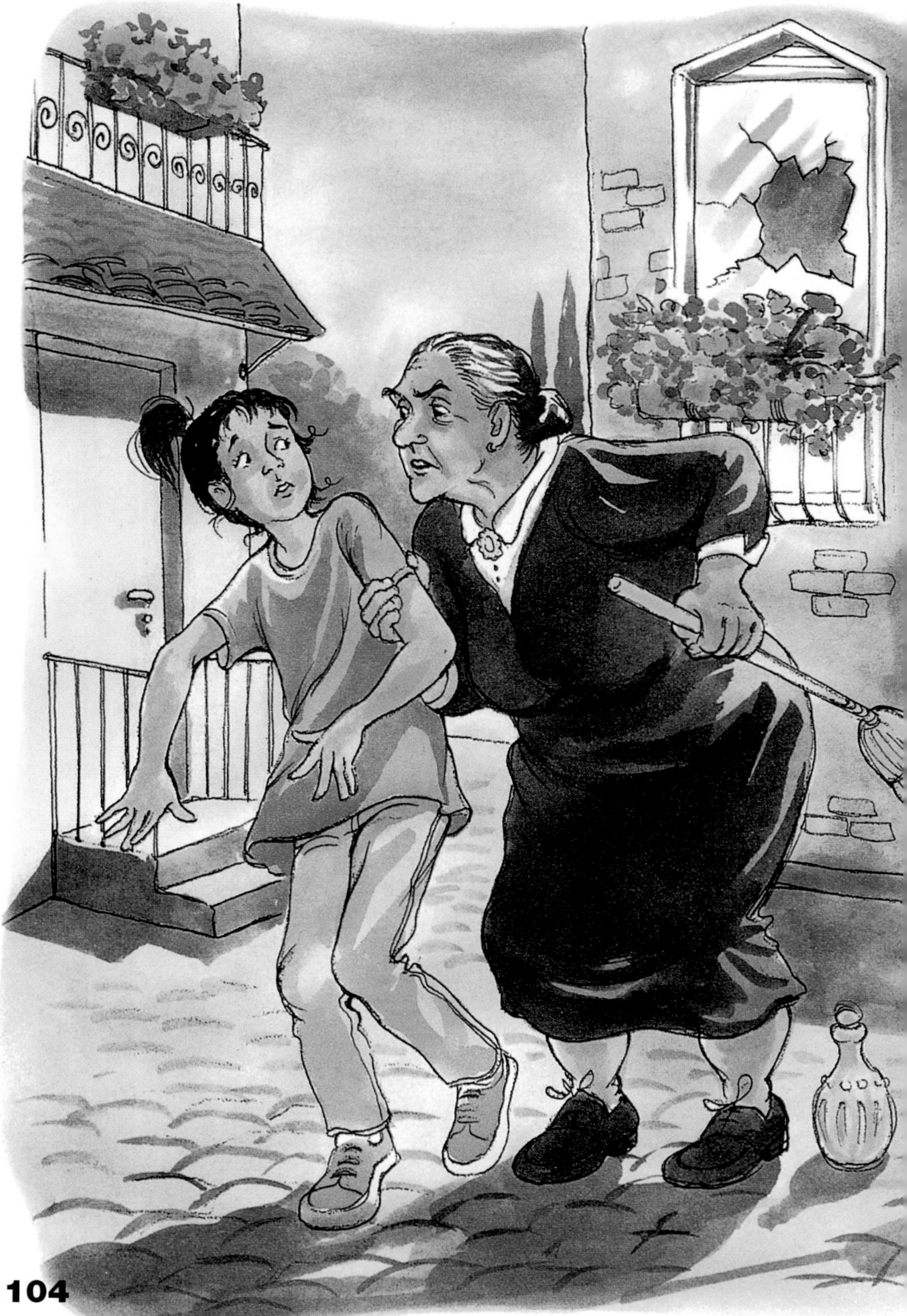

Carla Reads the Genie Book

Carla and Ott were in Rome. Ott had just made something happen the right way. He had wished for a window pane, and the pane came.

"I think I can get us out of here," Ott said. "But maybe I should call for help. I think I can do that now."

"All right," Carla said. "Call for help." Ott folded his arms and began to say things to himself. Then something began to fly across the sky. It began to dive at Ott. "Splat." It was a big wet, fat fish.

Carla began to laugh. Then she said, "I don't think you're a genie yet."

"You are right," Ott said. Then he held up a big book. "This is my school book," he said. "It tells you how to do things like a genie. Maybe we can read the book and find out how to ★ go home."⑤

"Good plan," Carla said. "Let's go to a

park and sit down in the shade."

So Ott and Carla went to a park. They sat near a little stream.

Carla said, "Let's flip to the back of the book. That part will tell how to do the hard tricks."

So Carla flipped to the back of the book. She stopped at the part that said, "How to Go Home."

"This is what we want," Carla said. She began to read the part out loud.

More next time

Carla Goes Home, Home, Home

Carla was reading from Ott's school book. She was reading a part that told what to do if you wanted to go home. Here is what the book said:

"If you want to go home, fold your arms. Then say the name of your street. Then say the name of your mother. Then say, 'Ib, bub, ib, bub, ib, bub, bibby. Bome, bome, bome. I want to go home, home, home.'"

When Carla was through reading, she said, "Did you hear that, Ott? It told you everything you have to do to get home."

Ott said, "That is too much to remember. I can't remember all of that."

"Oh, it's not so much. Here. I'll read it again, and I'll show you the things you have to do."

Carla began to read to herself. Then she folded her arms and said, "First you say the name of my street and the name of my mother.⑤ Here I go: Oak Street . . . Marta Flores."

Ott stood up and folded his arms. Then he said, "Oak Street . . . Marta Flores."

Carla said, "Here is what you say next: Ib, bub, ib, bub, ib, bub, bibby. Bome, bome, bome. I want to go home, home, home."

Suddenly, Carla was flying through the air. Thud. Now she was sitting on her front steps. She was still holding the genie school book.

"Wow," Carla said, "I did that trick all by myself." She began to think of the wonderful tricks she could play just by reading the genie book.

Suddenly, Carla remembered Ott. "Oh, my," she said. "He is not here. Maybe something bad happened to him. I better call for help."

Carla began flipping through the school book. She stopped at a part that told how to call for help.

More to come

Carla Calls for Help

Carla was reading a genie book. The book told about many tricks. One part told how to call for help. Carla was reading that part now. She wanted to call for another genie who could help her find Ott.

Carla stopped reading the part of the book that told how to call for help. Then she folded her hands and said some words. Suddenly, something appeared in the sky. It began to dive down. It was getting closer and closer. Then it stopped. It was an old genie. She stared at Carla. Then she said, "Don't tell me you called for help?"

"Yes, I did," Carla said. "I need help."

"But that is impossible," the old genie said. "You are a human. Everybody knows that a human is not smart. Everybody knows that it is impossible for a human to do the most simple trick." ⑤

"That is not so," Carla said. "I don't

know if I can do every trick in that book.
But I called you, and I did the other trick
I tried."

"That is impossible," the old genie said.

"I'll show you," Carla said.

She opened the book to the part that
told how to make a rock into water. After
she was through reading what the book
said, she found a big rock. She told the old
genie to hold the rock on top of her head.

Suddenly, the rock turned into water.
Splash. It flowed all over the old genie. She
began spitting water. She said, "How dare
you. How dare you do a thing like that to
me."

Carla said, "Don't get mad at me. I
called for help. I didn't call you so that we
could get in a fight. I need your help to
find Ott."

Stop

Carla Goes to Genie School

Carla told the old genie that she didn't want to fight with her. She needed her help.

"I will help," the old genie said.

Then the old genie stood on one foot. She said some words. "Poof." There was Ott standing next to the old genie.

"You're back," Carla said. She ran over and gave Ott a big hug.

"But I'm afraid he'll have to come back to school with me," the old genie said. "He is not doing well as a genie. I will try to send another genie. I will take Ott back to school with me."

"No," Carla said. "I don't want another genie. I want Ott."

"But he is not fit to be a genie," the old genie said. "He can't even find his way home."

"I don't care," Carla said. "I want him for my genie.⑤ He's the one who came out of the bottle when I rubbed it. And he's the genie I want."

"But he must go back to school," the old genie said.

"That's all right," Carla said. "I can go to school with him."

"Oh no," the old genie said. "You can't go to our school."

"Why not?" Carla asked.

"Because you are not a genie," the old genie said. "You are a human. And everybody knows that humans can't do very simple tricks."

"Don't say that," Carla said, "or I will turn a thousand rocks into water and you will have to swim home."

"All right, all right," the old genie said. "You can come to genie school, but I don't think you're going to like it."

"Poof." In an instant, Carla and Ott
were standing in front of the other children
in the genie school.

Stop

Carla Is the Best in Genie School

Ott and Carla and the old genie were in front of the children in the genie school. The old genie said, "This is Carla. She is going to work in this school just like the rest of you."

One of the boys said, "Not here. She can't stay here. She is only a human, and everybody knows that humans can't do any tricks."

Carla snapped her fingers. A rock appeared. She said to the boy who had just talked, "Sit on that rock."

The boy sat on the rock. Carla folded her arms and said some words to herself.

Splash. The boy was sitting in a pool of water.

"Ho, ho," the other children said. "She can do some good tricks. It will be fun to have her in school with us."

So Carla stayed in school. She worked as hard as any of the genies.⑤ And she was the best in the class. When the teacher told the children and Carla how to do a new trick, Carla was always the best at doing the trick. Then she would help the other girls and boys work on the new trick.

Every day, Carla went to school and worked on new tricks. Every day she became smarter and better at genie tricks. Soon, she was ready to become a genie. She was very proud. She was the only human in the genie school. And she was better than anybody else in school. In fact, her teacher said that she was the smartest one he ever had in school.

Then the big day came. This was the day that everyone in school took a vow to be a genie. After taking this vow, they became real genies and went to stay in a bottle.

This was a very big day for Carla, a very big day.

To be continued

Will Carla Take the Genie Vow?

The day had come for everyone in school to take a vow to be a genie. The old genie came to class that day. She had a ring for every new genie.

Before she gave out the rings, she stood in front of the class and said, "Today is your last day in this school. You have worked hard and now you are ready to leave. You are ready to take your place as a genie. But before you take your vow, remember this. It is not easy to be a genie. You must forget about the things that you want to do. You must think about your master. You must do only what your master wants you to do. Not all of you will have good masters. But once you take the genie vow, you must do what genies have done for ★ thousands and thousands of years.⑤ You must obey your master at all times. You must forget about yourself."

The old genie looked at Carla. Carla looked down. Then she began to cry. She felt very bad. She liked the genie school, but she didn't want to spend the rest of her life in a bottle. She didn't want to forget about herself and do what her master wanted her to do. She said, "I can't do it. I can't take the vow of a genie."

All of the children looked at her. The old genie patted her on the back. Then the old genie said, "We don't want you to take the vow. You are a human, and you should spend life as a human spends life. I once told you that you would not like genie school."

"But I did like it," Carla said. "I just can't take that vow."

"Carla," the old genie said, "we are very glad that you came to our school. You showed us a lot about humans. We won't feel bad if you don't take the vow. This vow is for genies, not for humans."

Carla wiped her eyes. All of the
children smiled. Carla could see that they
were not mad at her. She felt better now.

Stop

Carla and Ott Are Teachers

Carla had worked hard at the genie school. But she couldn't take the vow that the other genies took. She clapped as each new genie got a ring. And she clapped the hardest for Ott. He was the last genie to get a ring.

Then the old genie said, "Here are your jobs. She handed each genie a folded paper. The paper told where the genie would work as a genie. One genie was sent to Alaska. One genie went to China. One genie went to Japan. And one genie went to stay in a yellow bottle that belonged to a girl named Carla.

The genie who got that job was named Ott. Ott was a genie now. He could do all the genie tricks. He had passed all the tests. And he had taken his vow to do what his master wants him to do.⑤

Just when Ott was reading his note,

the teacher ran into the room. He told the old genie, "Five new bottles have been found. We're going to need more genies, but how are we going to train them? I am the only teacher, and I will have to go to a bottle now."

Carla said, "Wait. Ott and I can train the new genies. The school would have two teachers. That means the school could train more genies than it could with one teacher."

The old genie said, "That is a fine plan."

The teacher said, "Yes, that plan is good."

That's what happened.

Now lots of new genies are being trained. And the boys and girls in genie school have good teachers. Ott is a good teacher, because he remembers how hard it was for him to pick up new tricks. Carla is a good teacher because she is very smart.

And Ott and Carla are very, very happy.

And this is the end of the story.

The Van and the Vane

Kim did not spell well. When she made a note, she did not spell words the right way. Here is how Kim spelled the word **made: mad.** Here is how Kim spelled the word **van: vane.** Here is how she spelled the word **mat: mate.**

One day, Kim was going to leave her house and move to the other side of town. She had a lot of stuff to move. So she said, "I will call a van and have the van move my stuff to the other side of town."

So Kim looked in the phone book. But she did not look under the word **van**. She looked under the word **vane**. She talked to a woman who made vanes. These vanes are made to show you which way the wind is blowing. When the wind blows from the east, the vane turns to the east.⑤ When the wind blows from the west, the vane turns to the west.

Kim said to the woman, "I want the biggest one you have. How big is your biggest one?"

The woman on the phone said, "Our biggest one is ten feet long."

"That doesn't seem very big," Kim said. "How soon could you send it to my house?"

The woman said, "I can have it at your house in five minutes."

"Good," Kim said. "Send it right over."

Kim hung up the phone. Then she rushed around her house packing her things. Soon the door bell rang. Kim ran to the door. A woman was standing at the door. She was holding a big vane.

Kim said, "Where is your van?"

The woman said, "I came in a car."

Kim said, "Who is bringing the van?"

"What van?" the woman asked. "I came here with a vane."

Kim said, "What vane?"

The woman held up the vane and said, "This vane."

To be continued

The Truck and the Trunk

Kim had called the woman who made vanes. That woman was at Kim's door. But Kim didn't need a big vane to tell which way the wind was blowing. Kim needed a big van so that she could take her things to the other side of town.

The woman said, "You called me and told me to bring the biggest vane I had. Here it is. I will send you a bill for it."

The woman handed the vane to Kim. Then the woman left. Kim felt very mad. She tossed the big vane in the corner of the room and went back to the phone book. She said, "This time I will look up trucks. I will call for a truck."

Kim looked in the phone book. But she didn't look under the word truck. She looked under the word trunk.⑤ She called the man and said, "I need something to take my things to the other side of town."

The man said, "I think I have just what you need. Do you have a lot of things?"

"Yes," Kim said.

"That's fine," the man said. "I'll bring you something to hold lots of things."

"Swell," Kim said. "Send it over right now. I'm in a big rush."

As Kim waited for the man to come to her house, Kim piled all of her things near the door. She said, "When that truck gets here, I'll throw my stuff in it and I'll be on my way."

Soon the front door bell rang. Kim opened the door. She saw a man dragging a super big trunk. Kim said, "Where's the truck?"

The man said, "It's out on the street. Why do you ask?"

"What do you mean? I ask because I called for a truck."

The man looked very mad. "No," he said. "You called and asked for a trunk."

"What do I want with a trunk?" Kim said. "I need a truck, not a trunk."

"Well, you've got a trunk, because you called me and asked me to bring you a trunk. And I'm not leaving until you pay for this trunk. It sells for ninety dollars."

Kim got ninety dollars and gave it to the fat man. Then Kim tossed her trunk in the corner with her other things. Now she had a vane and a trunk.

Stop

A Man Brings False Teeth

Kim was mad. She wanted to take her things to a house on the other side of town. But she didn't have a truck. She sent for a van, but she got a vane. Then she sent for a truck and she got a trunk.

Kim picked up the phone book and said, "This time I will look up a rental car. I can't get all of my stuff into a rental car. But I will make two or three trips in the car. In that way, I will be able to get my stuff to the other side of town."

So Kim went through the phone book. Then she stopped to read a phone number. But she was not looking under the words rental car. She was looking under the words dental care. Kim was calling a man who made false teeth.⑤

When the man answered the phone, Kim said, "Hello. Do you have something I

can rent today? I'll just need it for one
day."

The man said, "You want to rent just
for the day? That's a strange thing to do."

"Do you have anything to rent?" Kim
said.

"Well, yes, I do," the man said. "It may
not fit, but I can bring it over."

"That will be fine," Kim said.

Soon the door bell rang. Kim opened
the door. The man was standing there
holding a set of false teeth.

Kim said, "Where's your car?"

"It's out on the street," the man said.
"And here are your false teeth. I'll let you
have them for ten dollars a day."

"I don't need teeth," Kim said. "I need
a car. That's why I called you. You said
that you would bring me a car."

"No, I didn't," the man said. "I told you I would bring you a set of false teeth."

Kim picked up the phone book. She said, "Look at this. I'll show you that your name is under rental car." Kim opened the book.

The man said, "That doesn't say rental car. It says dental care."

Now Kim had a vane and a trunk and a set of rented teeth.

More next time

Kim Moves Her Stuff in a Van

Kim was really mad. After the man left Kim with a set of false teeth, Kim picked up the phone book and tossed it out of the window. She shouted, "That book gets me in a lot of trouble."

A boy was passing by Kim's house. He stopped and picked up the phone book. He said, "Is this your book?"

"I just tossed it away," Kim said. "I can't find anything in it."

"What do you want to find?" the boy asked.

"I need a van to take my things to the other side of town."

"Here," the boy said. He walked over to Kim. He had already found the right place in the phone book. "Why don't you call this number? It says that they have very fast service every day."

So Kim called the number.⑤ She said to the ★ woman who answered the phone, "I don't want a vane. I don't need any trunks. And I have lots of teeth. I need a van. Do you have a van?"

"Yes," the woman said. "We'll send one right out to you."

And at last a van came to Kim's house. "It's about time," Kim said. And in no time Kim had loaded all of her stuff into the van. She loaded her bike and her bags and her skates and her vane and her trunk. She slipped her false teeth into her pocket. Then she got into the van.

And when she was ready to leave her house, the boy said, "I can go with you and help."

"Yes," Kim said. "You can come along and help me read the names of the streets. I am going to Jane Street. You can see to it that I don't end up on Jan Street or on Jame Street."

"Okay," the boy said. He rode in the front of the van with Kim. And he told Kim when they reached Jane Street. He was a big help. When he had helped Kim take all of her stuff from the van, Kim said, "I would like to give you something for helping me." And what do you think Kim gave him?

He now has a big vane in his back yard. He is very proud of that vane.

The end of the story

Ellen the Eagle

One day Ellen the eagle went on a long trip with her brother. Ellen and her brother didn't drive. They didn't go on a train. They flew. The day was very hot and very dry.

At last her brother said, "Let's stop flying. I need something to drink."

So Ellen and her brother landed on the hot, dry ground. But they did not see any lakes or any ponds. They walked around for a long time looking for water. Ellen's brother was shouting, "I need water. I can't stand this much longer."

The eagles kept looking and looking. All at once, Ellen saw a deep hole that was not very big around. She stuck her head down the hole. There was water in the bottom of that hole. Ellen bent over as far as she could, but she could not reach the water. The hole was not very wide.⑤ So

Ellen could not slide down and get the water.

Ellen called her brother. Her brother said, "I must have water. I must have water." He stuck his head down the hole and tried to reach the water, but he couldn't. Then he rolled over on the ground and began to shout, "I must have water."

"Stop that," Ellen said. "If we are smart, we can find out how to get that water from the hole."

Ellen began to think. Suddenly she jumped up. "Pick up some stones and drop them into the hole."

"How will that help us?" her brother asked.

"You will see," Ellen said. "Just start dropping stones into the hole."

So Ellen and her brother dropped stones into the hole. And every time a stone went to the bottom of the hole, the

water moved up a little bit. Up, up, up.
After Ellen and her brother had dropped
many stones, the water was near the top of
the hole.

The eagles could reach the water now.
So they drank and drank and drank. Then
they sat in the shade of a big tree.

Then Ellen's brother said, "Ellen, you
are a smart eagle, and you are the best
sister an eagle can have."

The end

Carl Tricks the Crow

Carl was a very smart mouse. He lived with three other mice. When the other mice played games, Carl sat. He would think and think. Then he would do something smart.

One year things got very bad for the mice. There was not much food, and all the mice were very hungry. They cried, and yelled, and shouted. They ran around and said, "What are we going to do? What are we going to do?"

One day they came to Carl and said, "Carl, we need food. You are very smart. Can you find some food for us?"

"I think so," Carl said.

Carl left the other mice and went out to find food. Soon he came to a big tree. A crow was sitting in that tree. And the crow had a very big chunk of cheese in his mouth.⑤ Carl said to himself, "The other mice and I could have a real meal if I could get the cheese from the crow." So Carl made up a plan for getting the cheese.

Then he said, "My, you are a good-looking crow. You have such pretty wings and such big black feathers."

The crow smiled, but he did not say anything. If he opened his mouth to say something, the cheese would fall from his mouth.

Carl said, "You have such big wings. I'll bet you can fly very far."

The crow smiled and held out his wings.

"Yes," Carl said. "And you have such good-looking legs. I'll bet you run fast with those legs."

The crow smiled and ran up and down the branch of the tree.

Carl said, "I'll bet you can sing well, too."

The crow shook his head no, but he didn't say a thing.

"Come on," Carl said. "Just sing a little bit for me. Come on, you big handsome crow."

The crow smiled and opened his mouth. "Caw, caw," he said. And as he did, the chunk of cheese fell from his mouth. Carl grabbed the cheese and waved to the crow. "You are good at singing, and you are very, very kind. Thank you for this cheese. Thank you very much."

The crow started to tell Carl that he didn't mean to drop the cheese, but Carl kept talking. "I don't think I've ever seen a crow that was as handsome or as kind as you are."

The crow smiled. And Carl went home

with the cheese. That night he and the other mice had a fine meal. The other mice said, "Carl, you are very smart."

This story is over.

The Turtle and the Frog

Once there was an egg. This egg was on the shore of a pond. It was in the sand. The sun was shining, and the egg was getting hotter and hotter.

Then one day something came out of the egg. Did a chicken come out of the egg? No. Did a little duckling come out of the egg? No. What came out of the egg? A turtle.

That turtle did not know that he was a turtle. He came out of the egg and looked around. Things looked good to him. The sun felt hot. That felt good. He walked to the pond. The water felt good. He went for a swim. That was fun. Then he sat on a log. He grabbed a fly and ate it. That was good.

Then he saw a frog. The frog got up on the log.⑤ Then the frog said, "You are funny-looking."

The turtle did not know what to say. He had never really looked at himself. He didn't feel funny-looking. Now he felt a little sad. He said to the frog, "You look good."

"Yes," the frog said and smiled. "I am good. Watch this." The frog jumped way up and then—splash. He landed in the water.

"Wow," the turtle said. "I like that. I think I'll jump way up and land in the water."

So the turtle tried to jump way up. But he didn't go way up. He slid off the log and landed in the water. When he came up, the frog said, "Ho, ho. You are funny. You can't even jump. Ho, ho."

The little turtle was not going "ho, ho." He was feeling very, very sad. Before he met that frog, things had seemed good to him. But now the pond did not look pretty,

and the sun did not feel good. Everything
seemed sad.

More to come

Flame the Snake

A little turtle was very sad because he could not do things a frog did. The frog could jump way up. But the turtle could not jump at all. The frog got out of the pond and yelled, "Come up here to the land. I want to take a good look at you."

So the turtle came out of the pond. He was wet all over. So the frog could not see that the turtle had tears on his cheeks.

"Ho, ho," the frog said. "You look like a big toenail. You look like the foot of a horse. You look like a joke." The frog jumped up and down on the turtle's shell. "Come on," the frog said. "Take off this hard coat and let me wear it. Then I will look like a toenail."

"I can't take it off," the turtle said. ⑤ "That hard coat is part of me."

The frog started to laugh. He laughed

so hard that tears were running down his
cheeks. He laughed until the ground around
him was wet. And then he laughed some
more.

Suddenly, he stopped laughing.
Suddenly, he yelled, "Get out of here.
Flame the snake is coming." And
then—zip—the frog jumped into the pond.

Before the turtle could get into the
pond, a long, fat snake came sliding out of
the weeds. The snake slid up to the turtle
and smiled.

"Hello," the snake said. "My name is
Flame. And I need something to eat. Are
you good to eat?"

"I don't think so," the turtle said. "I
don't think I'm good at anything."

"That is too bad," the snake said. "But
maybe you could help me. Have you seen
any frogs around here?"

The turtle looked at the smiling snake.
He looked at the snake's big mouth. Then
the turtle told a lie.

"No," the turtle said, "I have not seen
any frogs around here."

To be continued

Flame the Snake Is a Sneak

Flame the snake was looking for something to eat. The turtle said, "No, I have not seen any frogs around here."

Flame smiled and started to slide back into the weeds. Then that snake stopped and said, "I will be back."

The turtle said to himself, "I don't like that snake. I think she is a sneak. I think I will leave." The turtle walked into the pond and began to swim around. Then the frog came over to him. The frog said, "What did Flame say to you?"

The turtle said, "She said that she wanted something to eat."

The frog asked, "Did she say what she wanted to eat?"

"Yes," the turtle said. "She told me that she wanted to eat a frog."

"That is bad," the frog said. "That is very, very bad." The frog jumped from the pond and sat ★ on an old log.⑤ He shook his head. "That is bad," he said again. "Flame is very strong. Flame is very fast. And she is a sneak. She gives me a big scare."

Just then, a big mouth shot up to the log. Snap. It was Flame's mouth. And it just missed the frog. The frog jumped from the log, but he landed in the tall weeds. Flame smiled and began to slide into the weeds.

Flame said, "Frogs can't jump very well when they are in the weeds. I think I will have my lunch now. I think my lunch is here in the weeds."

"Save me," the frog yelled. "I can't get away from that snake. Save me."

The turtle shouted, "I will save you."

The turtle began to walk as fast as he could go. Flame the snake stopped.

"My, my," Flame said. "I see a walking toadstool." Flame was still smiling. "Get out of my way, you silly-looking thing, or I will eat you, too."

The turtle said, "If you don't stop sliding after that frog, I'll bite you on the nose."

Flame smiled and turned away. She seemed to be going back to the log. But suddenly—snap. Like a shot, her mouth came at the turtle.

This story is not over.

A Snake Must Do What Snakes Do

Flame the snake was after the turtle. Her mouth came at the turtle like a shot. The turtle was not fast like a frog, so he could not jump out of the way. The turtle pulled his head into his shell. And just then —bong—the snake's mouth hit the shell.

"Ow, ow," Flame yelled. "My tooth, my tooth. I think I broke my tooth on that hard shell." Flame was sliding this way and that way. "Ow, ow."

The turtle said, "That would not happen if you were a good snake. But you are a sneak."

The snake said, "You are silly. Everybody knows that snakes are sneaks. I am a snake, so I have to be sneaky."

"No," the turtle said. "You do not have to be sneaky. You could be anything you want."

The snake said, "You're nuts.⑤ You

can't be anything you want. Could you jump like a frog? Could you fly like a bird?"

"No," the turtle said, "I can't do those things."

Flame said, "Then why do you think I can be anything I want to be?"

The turtle said, "Maybe you are right. I can't do things that frogs do. I can only do what turtles do. You are a snake, so you must do what snakes do."

"Thank you," Flame said, and smiled. "If you will get out of my way, I'll do what snakes do. I'll go into the weeds and have a frog for lunch."

"Yes," the turtle said. The turtle stepped to one side and the snake began to slide into the weeds. The turtle was sad, but the turtle felt that Flame must do what snakes do.

This is almost the end.

The Frog and the Turtle
and the Snake Get Along

Flame the snake was sliding into the weeds. She was going after the frog.

"Save me, save me," the frog yelled. "Please save me from this snake."

Suddenly, the turtle took a big bite out of the snake's tail. "Ow, ow," the snake yelled. "Why did you do that?" Flame asked. "I must do what snakes do."

The turtle said, "I have to do what turtles do."

Then Flame called, "Frog, oh frog. Come out here." The frog hopped out of the weeds. He looked scared. Flame looked at him and began to slide after him.

"Stop," the turtle called. "Stop, or I will bite your tail again."

So Flame stopped. Then the turtle said, "You can be a sneak when you are not around me or this frog. But you cannot be a sneak around us." ⑤

Flame said, "Can I be a sneak when I go to hunt rats near the farm?"

"Yes," the turtle said.

Flame asked, "Can I be a sneak and eat a frog?"

"No," the turtle said. "You must be good to that frog."

Flame looked sad. "I will be good," she said.

So from that day on, the frog and the turtle and the snake got along very well. The frog did what frogs do. He jumped and swam and went "Croak, croak" at night. But that frog did not make fun of turtles any more.

When Flame was not near the pond, she did what snakes do. She would sneak and she would eat many things. But when she was around the frog and the turtle, she was a good snake.

Now the turtle felt good again. He liked to watch the frog jump and watch the snake slide along the ground. He liked the hot sun and the cool water. He liked to be alive.

This is the end.

The Boy Who Yelled "Wolf"

There once was a boy who had a very big job. Every day he took a flock of sheep up the side of the mountain. His job was to watch the sheep and keep them safe. He had to watch for wolves and for mountain lions.

But this boy was not a hard worker. He didn't like his job. One day, he said to himself, "I am tired of watching sheep. I want to have some fun." He began to think of ways to have fun. Then he smiled and said, "I think I'll run into town and play a good joke on the people. I will tell them that a big wolf has come to eat the sheep. They will run back here to get the wolf. Then I will tell them that there is no wolf. That will be a good joke." ⑤

So the boy went to town and began to shout, "Help, help. A big wolf is eating the sheep."

The people ran to the flock of sheep. When they got there, the boy started to laugh. "Ha, ha," he said. "I played a good joke on you. There is no wolf here."

The boy's father said, "That is not a good joke. Some day a wolf will come to the flock. But nobody will believe you when you yell, 'Wolf, wolf.'"

The next week the boy got tired of watching sheep again. So he went to town and yelled, "Wolf, wolf. A big wolf is eating the sheep." The people in town ran to the flock. But when they got there, the boy began to laugh. "Ha, ha. I played a good joke on you."

Again, his father told him that someday a wolf would come, but nobody would listen to the boy when he shouted, "Wolf, wolf."

The next week, the boy was sitting on the side of the mountain when he saw something chasing a sheep. It was a big wolf. "I must get the people," the boy yelled, and he ran to town as fast as he could go.

"Wolf, wolf," he yelled. "A big wolf is after the sheep."

But the people did not run to save the sheep. They laughed at the boy. They said, "You can't fool us with your jokes."

"I am not joking," the boy said, but the people would not believe him.

The wolf ate some sheep. But after that day, the boy did his job very well. He did not get tired of watching the sheep. And he never yelled, "Wolf, wolf" when there was no wolf.

This is the end.

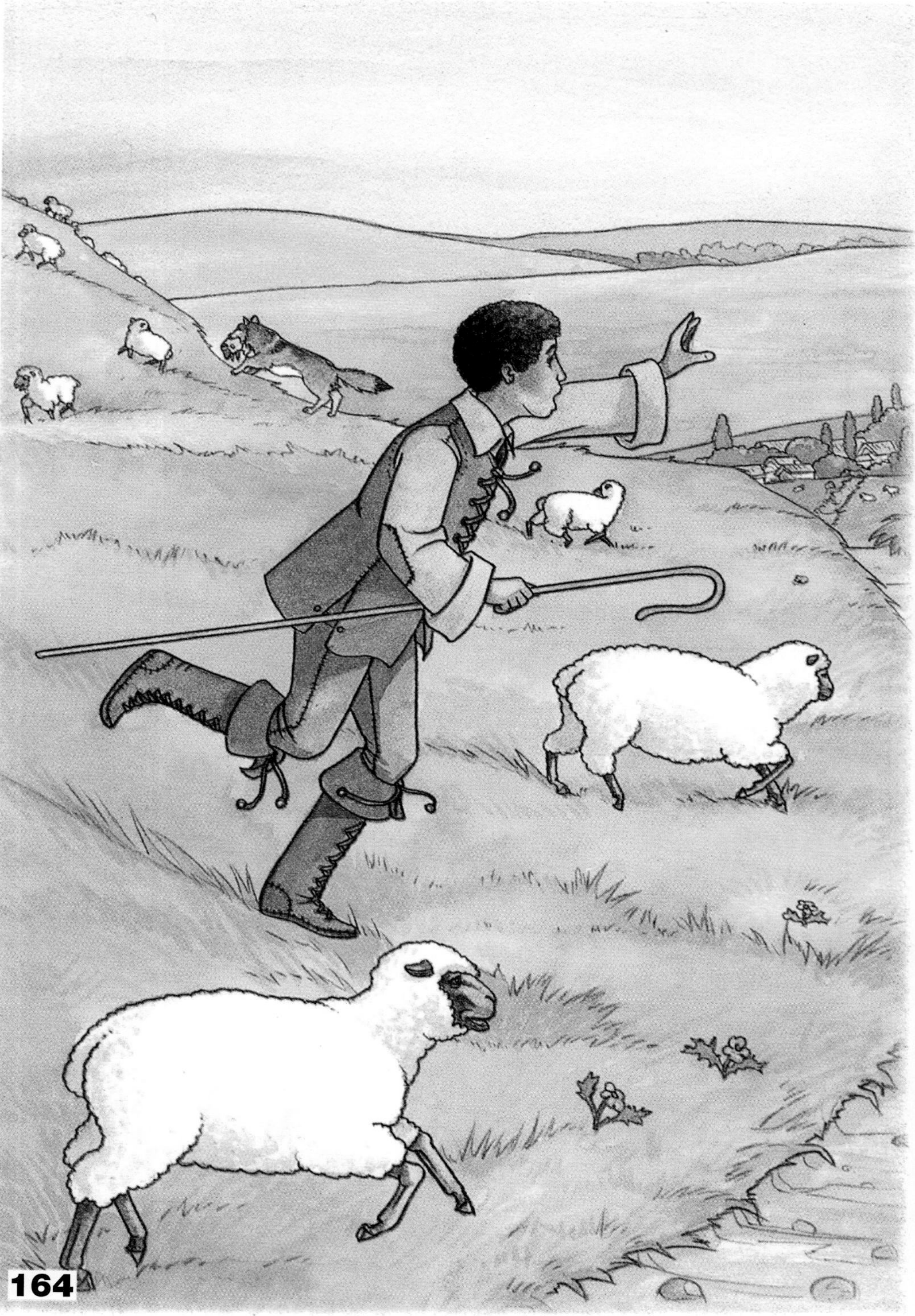

1

The Rabbit and the Turtle

The rabbit was the fastest animal in the woods. She said, "Ha, ha. I am so fast that nobody can beat me in a race." All of the other animals got mad at the rabbit. But none of the other animals raced with the rabbit because they knew she could beat them.

One day the rabbit was jumping around and saying, "Ha, ha. I am so fast that nobody can beat me in a race." She ran around and around, making a lot of dust fly up into the air. The other animals were mad.

Then one of the animals said, "I will race with you." It was the turtle, and he was the slowest animal in the woods.

The rabbit laughed and laughed. "You want to race with me," she said. "That is a joke. I am so fast that I could run a mile before you take one step."⑤ The rabbit ran around the turtle a few times, making a lot of dust fly up into the air.

The turtle said, "I will race with you. And if I win the race, you will have to stop telling everybody how fast you are."

"And what if I win the race?" the rabbit said. "What will you do, Mr. Turtle?"

The turtle said, "I will ride you around the woods on my back. I will take you any place you want to go."

"This will be fun," the rabbit said. "This will be an easy race for me to win."

So the animals got ready for the race. The rabbit and the turtle would have a long, long race from one side of the woods to the other. They would race over the path and across the stream and over the hill. The first animal to reach the big rock on the other side of the woods would win the race.

The rabbit and the turtle lined up. Then
the owl said, "Go." The rabbit went down
the path like a shot. She made so much dust
that the turtle couldn't see. The ant and
the other animals said, "It looks like the
rabbit will win this race."

More to come

2

The Rabbit and the Turtle

All of the other animals wanted to see the turtle beat the rabbit in a race. The rabbit had told everybody that she would stop telling how fast she was if the turtle beat her. But the rabbit seemed far too fast for the turtle. The rabbit went flying over the path and over the stream. Soon she was at the hill. She stopped to look back. All she could see was a cloud of dust. "Ho, ho," she said. "That turtle must be a mile behind me. He cannot win this race."

So the rabbit sat down under a tree. She closed her eyes and leaned back. And the first thing you know she was sound asleep.

The turtle didn't stop when the rabbit got far ahead of him. The turtle kept going as fast as he could go. He just kept going and going.⑤ He said to himself, "I'll just keep on going, ★ and I'll beat that rabbit."

After a while, the turtle came to the stream. He crossed the stream and started up the hill. He could see the big rock on the other side of the woods. And he could see the rabbit. The rabbit was still sleeping under the tree.

The turtle said to himself, "I'll just keep on going."

And he did. He went past the rabbit. He was getting closer and closer to the big rock. A bunch of animals were waiting by the rock. When they saw the turtle coming up the side of the hill, they started to shout, "Come on, turtle. You can do it."

They yelled louder and louder as the turtle got closer and closer to the big rock. When the turtle was only a few feet from the rock, they were yelling so loud that they woke up the rabbit.

"What's this?" she said. She looked around and saw the turtle near the rock. When that rabbit saw what was happening, she began to run so fast that you couldn't see her. She went so fast that the grass bent over, and the dust cloud was so thick that you couldn't see the sun. She ran so fast that the other animals just looked at her with big eyes.

But she didn't win the race. The turtle stepped past the big rock just before the rabbit shot by in a cloud of dust.

Now all of the animals are happy because the rabbit doesn't tell everybody how fast she is. And the rabbit is a little smarter than she was. She knows that it takes more than speed to win a race. You have to keep trying.

The end

171

The Lion and the Mouse

There once was a lion who lived in the jungle. The lion was the king of all the animals in the jungle. He was big, and he was mean. If he said, "Get out of my way," the other animals got out of his way. If he said, "Come here," the other animals came to the lion.

One day a little mouse came up to the lion. The mouse said, "I want to be your friend. I am just a little mouse, but I will be a good friend."

The lion laughed. "Ha, ha," he said. "What do I need with a little friend like you? What can you do for me? I am the strongest animal in the jungle. I am the best hunter. I am king of all the animals."

The little mouse said, "But I will be a good friend." ⑤

The lion laughed so hard that the mouse fell down. Then the lion said, "Go

away, you silly little mouse." So the mouse
went away. He had a tear in his eye. He
wanted to be friends with the lion.

Then one day the lion got a big thorn
in his paw. He roared with pain.
"Roooaaar." He called the other animals. He
said, "Get that thorn out of my paw."

The elephant tried, but he could not get
a good hold on the thorn. He said, "I am
sorry, king lion, but I cannot get that thorn
out of your paw."

The alligator tried to get a hold on the
thorn with his teeth, but he could not. He
said, "I am sorry, king lion, but I cannot
get that thorn out of your paw."

The other animals tried, but none of
them could get the thorn out. Then, after
the other animals left, that big king lion
started to cry. He said, "Ow. My paw is
sore, and nobody can help me. Nobody can
get that thorn out."

The little mouse came up to the lion and said, "I can get that thorn out. I am little. I have little paws, so I can get a hold on that thorn." And he did. He grabbed the thorn and gave it a jerk. And the thorn came out.

The lion began to cry. "It feels good to get the thorn out," he said. "Little mouse, you are my best friend."

So if you go to the jungle and you see a little mouse, be good to that little mouse, because he has a friend. His friend is the king of all the animals in the jungle.

This is the end.

Casey the Rabbit

Casey was a rabbit. He was a good rabbit, but he liked to play tricks on the other animals in the woods. Most of all he liked to play tricks on a mean fox.

When the fox would try to steal hens from a barn, Casey the rabbit would sneak up in back of the fox and yell, "Boo." The fox would jump, and the chickens would start running around. The farmer would hear the chickens and shoot at the fox.

When the fox would try to steal honey from a tree, Casey would sneak up in back of the fox and throw a rock at the bees. The bees would get mad and they would chase the fox into the lake.

One day the fox said, "I must get rid of that rabbit."

So he made a trap for Casey. He put a big salad on a path in the woods.⑤ When Casey stopped to eat the salad, the fox grabbed Casey.

The fox was very happy. He said, "You will never yell 'Boo' when I am stealing chickens. I am going to get rid of you."

Casey said, "I don't care what you do to me, but please don't throw me into the thorn bushes."

The fox said, "Why don't you want me to throw you into the thorn bushes?"

And Casey told the fox, "Look at the thorns in the thorn bushes. Hang me, or shoot me, or throw me in the lake. But please don't throw me into those thorn bushes."

The fox looked at the big thorns on the bushes. Then he said, "I will throw you into the thorn bushes." And he gave Casey a big heave.

The fox said to himself, "That was a good way to get rid of that rabbit."

But suddenly, Casey began to laugh from the thorn bushes. "Ha ha, ho ho, he, he, he.

I'm Casey the rabbit and you can't hurt me."

Then Casey said, "I love thorn bushes, you silly fox." He jumped around in the thorns.

The fox was very mad because Casey had tricked him. And Casey was very happy. He laughed and said, "Ha ha, ho ho, he, he, he. I'm Casey the rabbit, and you can't hurt me."

The end

Mr. Hall

Mr. Hall had a nice home and a nice car. He had lots of cash. Everybody said that he was a fine man.

But there was something about Mr. Hall that only a few people knew. He was afraid of dogs. When a dog got near him, he would begin to shake. He would start to think that the dog was going to come after him. Mr. Hall had been afraid of dogs from the time he was a little boy. But he couldn't help his fear. The bigger a dog was, the more fear Mr. Hall had. Mr. Hall stayed away from dogs whenever he could.

But then something strange happened. Mr. Hall was on a ship. He was on his way to Japan. One day he was walking on the deck of the ship when he saw a dog. This dog was nearly as big as a horse.⑤ When Mr. Hall saw him, Mr. Hall got a chill up and down his back. Mr. Hall stopped and began to shake.

For the next three days, Mr. Hall was afraid to go on the deck of the ship. He was so afraid of the dog that he stayed in his room. But he left his room on the fourth day. He was reading a book when suddenly the ship jerked. Mr. Hall fell from his chair. He tried to get up, but the ship was leaning to the side. People were yelling, "Help, help. The ship is sinking."

Mr. Hall opened the door to his room. He went up the stairs to the deck. People were screaming. The ship was sinking.

Mr. Hall jumped into the water. Mr. Hall looked for something to hang on to. He swam and swam. Then he saw something—a big raft. He got on the raft and sat down. He looked around for the ship, but the ship was gone. He looked for other people, but he couldn't see anybody.

He looked and looked. And then, at last, he saw something swimming in the sea. It was that big, mean-looking dog. "I hope he doesn't come here," Mr. Hall said to himself. But the dog swam closer to the raft.

Then the dog tried to get on the raft. Mr. Hall sat on the other side of the raft. He was looking at the dog and shaking with fear.

More to come

The Dog Saves Mr. Hall

Mr. Hall was sitting on one side of the raft watching the dog. The dog was trying to get on the raft. At last he did. He shook himself and drops of water went flying. Mr. Hall did not take his eyes from the dog. The dog looked at Mr. Hall. Then he sat down. He was even bigger and meaner-looking than he seemed on the ship.

Mr. Hall sat on the other side of the raft for a long time. Then Mr. Hall saw a tin of crackers floating in the sea. He reached for it. Then he opened the tin and ate one of the crackers. The dog was looking at him. Mr. Hall began to think that the dog would eat him if he got hungry. So Mr. Hall tossed some crackers to the dog. The dog sniffed the crackers and then looked up at Mr. Hall. ⑤

"Go on and eat them," Mr. Hall said.

That was the first time he had ever talked to a dog.

The dog ate the crackers.

All day, Mr. Hall sat on one side of the raft and the dog sat on the other. Then, when the sun was setting, Mr. Hall saw a ship. He stood up and began to shout as loud as he could. "Here we are. Here we are," he shouted. The ship came closer and closer. And Mr. Hall kept shouting, "Here we are."

Now the ship was very close. Mr. Hall could see people on the deck. He could hear the sound of a band playing. He could hear people laughing and talking, but he could not shout any more. He had shouted too hard, and now he couldn't make loud sounds. "Help," he said, but nobody could hear him.

Mr. Hall was watching the ship go by,

and he was thinking this: "If that ship doesn't pick me up, I'll never be found. I will die out here in the middle of the sea. And that ship is so close I can almost reach it. If only the people could hear me."

Suddenly, Mr. Hall looked at that big dog and said, "Speak, speak."

The dog lifted his head. "Woo, woo." Out came a big, deep bark. It boomed out across the sea. "Woo, woo."

"Speak," Mr. Hall said again.

"Woo, woooo," the dog answered.

Now people on the deck were looking over the side of the ship. They were waving. "Hello," they were yelling. They saw Mr. Hall. Mr. Hall threw his arms around that dog and gave him a big hug.

Mr. Hall still lives in a nice house. He still has a nice car and a lot of cash. But there is one thing that is not the same about him.

He shares his house with his best
friend, a big, mean-looking dog. He loves
that dog.

The end

The Prince and the Tramp

There once was a prince. The prince always dressed in fine clothes. He had a gold crown and a long robe and red shoes. When the prince walked down the streets of the city, everybody would say, "We love the prince. He is so handsome."

When the prince was hungry, people would bring food to him. Then the prince would say to himself, "Everybody loves me."

When the prince was tired of walking, people would give him a horse to ride.

One day the prince met a tramp. This tramp did not have a gold crown, or a long robe, or red shoes. This tramp did not have any shoes. He had an old shirt with holes in it. But that tramp looked just like the prince.

The tramp said, "How strange. You look just like me."

The prince said, "Let us have some fun. ⑤

I will dress like you, and you will dress like ★ me."

So the prince put on the tramp's clothes, and the tramp put on the gold crown and the long robe and the red shoes. The tramp looked just like the prince. The tramp left the prince and walked down the street. And what do you think happened?

All the people looked at the tramp and said, "We love the prince."

A man came up to the tramp and said, "If you are tired of walking, you may have my horse."

A lady came up to the tramp and said, "You must be hungry. Come to my house and I will give you a big meal."

But the real prince did not have a good time. When he walked on the streets of the city, people said, "Get out of here, you tramp."

The prince was hungry. He wanted

something to eat. So he went up to a man and said, "I am hungry. Give me something to eat."

But the man said, "Get out of here, you tramp."

The prince was sad. He said to himself, "I didn't know how hard it is to be a tramp."

The real prince met the tramp the next day. The prince said, "You will come and live with me. You will never be a tramp again." So the prince took the tramp home.

And years later, the prince became king. He never forgot the day that he was a tramp. He tried to help all of the tramps in the city. He said, "The people love me because I have fine clothes. I will give the tramps nice clothes so the people will love them, too." And that's what the good king did.

The end

In the Land of Peevish Pets

Jean was very sad. Her dad would not let her have a pet dog. She said to herself, "I will go to sleep tonight. And I will sleep so hard that maybe I will go to a land that is far away. Maybe I will go to a land where I can have all the pets I want."

So Jean went to bed. She kept telling herself to sleep very hard. "Sleep hard," she said to herself.

And what do you think happened? She went to sleep and began to sleep very hard. She went into the deepest sleep there ever was. She slept and slept. And in her sleep she began to have a dream. There were lots of pets in her dream, but they were not like any pets that Jean had ever seen before. There were funny green animals with big hands and red feet.⑤ There were little bugs that talked. There were strange trees that seemed to be singing. And right in the

middle of her dream was an old wizard.
"Ho, ho," the wizard said to her. "What is
your name?"

"Jean," she answered.

"Well, Jean," he said, "I hope you have
a fine time here in the land of peevish pets.
But you must remember this rule: All little
crumps are mean."

"What are little crumps?" Jean asked.

"That doesn't matter," the wizard
answered. "Just remember the rule: All little
crumps are mean."

Jean said, "I'll remember that rule: All
crumps are mean."

"No, no," the wizard said. "All <u>little</u>
crumps are mean."

"I've got it," Jean said. "But what and
when . . . ."

The wizard was gone, and Jean was all
alone in the land of peevish pets.

More to come

Jean Meets a Mean Crump

Jean was in the land of peevish pets. She was trying to remember the rule the wizard had told her about crumps. What was that rule?

Jean saw an animal that looked like a frog. She said, "Are you a little crump?"

The animal said, "Gump, gump."

She spotted another animal. It looked like a ball of pink hair. She said, "Are you a little crump?"

The animal answered, "Wup, wup."

Jean asked other animals if they were crumps. But she did not find one crump. Then she said, "I think I will sit down and rest."

Just then, she saw two chairs. One chair was big and the other was little. She said, "I will sit in the little chair."

Just as she was getting ready to sit down, the chair said, "Crump, crump." When it said "Crump," she jumped. And she jumped just in time.⑤ The chair began to run after her.

"That little chair is a little crump," she said. The crump was swinging its arms. It was trying to bite her. She ran as fast as she could go. Suddenly she stopped. The wizard was standing in front of her. She said, "I don't like this place. Get me out of here."

The wizard laughed. He said, "You can't leave this place until you know sixteen rules. You already know one rule. Here is the next rule: If you say, 'Away, away,' a mean crump will go away."

Jean said, "I think I have that rule. If you say, 'Away, away,' a crump will go away."

"No," the wizard yelled. "A <u>mean</u> crump will go away."

Jean said, "But what and when . . . ."

The wizard was gone again. The little crump was sneaking up behind Jean. She turned around and tried to remember what to do, but she couldn't remember the rule.

Tell Jean how to make the mean crump go away.

Jean yelled, "Away, away." What do you think happened? That's right. The little mean crump went away.

More next time

Jean Follows a Dusty Path

Jean was having a strange dream. In her dream, a wizard told her that she must know sixteen rules before she could leave the place in her dream. She already knew a rule about little crumps: All little crumps are mean. She also knew a rule about getting rid of mean crumps. After you say that rule, you can turn this page around and read it.

If you say, "Away, away," a mean crump will go away.

Jean said to herself, "I will walk and walk until I find a way out of this silly place. I wish that wizard was here."

Just then, the wizard popped out from behind a tree. He said, "If you are going to walk around, remember this rule: Every dusty path leads to the lake."

Jean said, "Thank you. I can remember that rule. Every path leads to the lake." ⑤

"No," the wizard said. "Every <u>dusty</u> path leads to the lake."

Jean said the rule to herself. Then she turned to the wizard and said, "But what and when . . . ."

The wizard was gone.

Jean said, "I think I will go to the lake. What was the rule about going to the lake?"

Tell Jean the rule. Say it loud so that she can hear it.

"Thank you," Jean said. "Every dusty path leads to the lake."

So Jean went down a dusty path. Soon she came to the lake. But she didn't like the lake. The water was pink and there were funny animals all around the lake. She said, "I will leave this lake." So she started to walk back down a dusty path.

Do you think that dusty path led away from the lake?

What's the rule?

The path led right back to the lake. Why?

Yes, the rule says that every dusty path leads to the lake.

Jean tried to leave the lake by taking another dusty path. Where do you think that path led? Why?

Yes, the rule says that every dusty path leads to the lake. That path was dusty, so it led right back to the lake.

To be continued

Jean Follows a Rocky Path

Jean was mad. And she was tired. She was trying to leave the lake. She walked down dusty paths, but they led right back to the lake.

Tell Jean the rule about dusty paths. After you say the rule, turn this page around and read it.

Every dusty path leads to the lake.

Jean said, "I wish that wizard was around here."

Just then the wizard appeared. He said, "I see that you know the rule about the dusty paths. Now I will tell you the rule about the rocky paths. Every rocky path leads to the mountain."

"I can remember that rule," Jean said. "Every rocky path leads to the mountain."

"Very good remembering," the wizard said. "Soon you will know all sixteen rules."

Jean said, "But what and when . . . ."

Again the wizard was gone. Jean said,
"I want to go to the mountain.⑤ But I can't
remember which path to take."

Tell Jean the rule about the paths that
go to the mountain.

"Oh, thank you," Jean said. She took a
rocky path and soon she came to a big
mountain. But there were crumps all around
the mountain. And some of them were little.
What do you know about little crumps?

Jean said, "Oh, dear. There's a rule
about how to get rid of mean crumps, but
I can't remember that rule."

The mean crumps were starting to run
after Jean. Help Jean out. Tell her what to
do to make the mean crumps go away.

Jean said, "Away." Did the crumps go
away? Why not?

Jean said, "Go away." Did the crumps
go away? Why not?

Jean said, "Away, away." Did the

crumps go away. Why? What's the rule?
After you say the rule, turn this page
around and read the rule.

will go away.

If you say, "Away, away," a mean crump

More in the next story

Jean Looks for Food

Jean was dreaming about a strange place. She was at the mountain in the land of peevish pets. And she was very hungry. She said, "I wish I had something to eat, and I wish the wizard was here."

Just then the wizard appeared. He said, "You may eat all you want, but remember this rule: Red food is good to eat. See if you can say that rule."

Jean said, "Red food is good to eat."

The wizard said, "Good remembering."

Jean said, "I will remember that rule. But what and when . . . ."

The wizard was gone again. Jean said to herself, "That is strange. Every time I say 'But what and when,' the wizard goes away."

Jean looked around and found lots of food. There was food on the ground. There was food on the side of the mountain. There was a bowl of yellow ice cream right in front of her.⑤ Should she eat that yellow ice cream?

How do you know?

Tell Jean the rule before she tries to eat that ice cream.★

Jean saw big white grapes on a vine. Should she eat those white grapes?

How do you know?

Tell Jean the rule before she tries to eat them.

Jean saw a red banana. Should she eat that red banana?

How do you know?

Tell Jean the rule.

Jean did not think that the banana looked very good, but she took a bite out of it.

"Wow," she said. "This is the best banana I have ever had." She ate that banana.

Then she found another banana. That banana was yellow. Should she eat that banana?

How do you know?

Tell Jean the rule.

Jean dropped the yellow banana and picked up a red banana. She began eating it.

This is not the end.

Jean Eats Red Bananas

Let's see how much you remember.

What is the name of the land that Jean was dreaming about?

How many rules did she have to know before she could leave this land?

She knew a rule about little crumps. What did she know about all little crumps?

What do you do to make a mean crump go away?

What kind of path would you take if you wanted to go to the lake?

What kind of path would you take if you wanted to go to the mountain?

What kind of food is good to eat?

Jean had eaten a red banana, and it was very good. She picked up another red banana and ate it. Then she ate another red banana. When she had eaten the third red banana, she looked at her hand. It had red stripes on it. Her other hand had red stripes, too.⑤

She said, "What is happening to me?"
She looked at her legs. They had red
stripes. Her feet had red stripes. She had
red stripes all over herself.

She shouted, "Where is that wizard?"

"Here I am," the wizard said, and
stepped out from behind a tree.

Jean asked, "Why do I have red stripes
all over myself?"

The wizard answered, "There is a rule
about red bananas. If you eat three red
bananas, you get red stripes."

Jean said, "Why didn't you tell me that
rule before? Look at me. I have red stripes
all over. I don't want to have red stripes."

"But now you know another rule," the
wizard said. "That is good."

Jean said, "But what and when . . . ."
Suddenly, the wizard disappeared. Jean was
all alone again. She began to rub her arm
to get rid of the red stripes. But they

wouldn't rub off.

She was very sad. Suddenly something said, "Crump, crump." She turned around and saw a little crump coming after her. Tell Jean how to make that crump go away.

Jean said, "Away, away." And the crump went away. But Jean still had red stripes.

She said, "I hope I remember that rule about eating three red bananas." Help Jean say the rule.

More about Jean's stripes next time

Jean Wants to Get Rid of
the Red Stripes

Jean was having a dream. What was the name of the land in her dream?

Was Jean having a good time?

Why did Jean have red stripes all over herself?

What's the rule about three red bananas?

She said, "Oh, I wish the wizard was here." Just as she said the words, the wizard appeared. Then Jean said, "What's the rule about getting rid of all these red stripes?"

The wizard said, "Here's the rule: If you jump in the lake, the stripes will disappear. Can you say that rule?"

Jean tried to say the rule, but she got mixed up. Help her say the rule.

After Jean said the rule, she said, "But what and when . . . ."

The wizard disappeared.

Jean said, "Well, I had better go to the lake."

Jean saw a rocky path. She ran down it as fast as she could go.⑤ Where did the rocky path lead?

Tell Jean the rule about every rocky path.

When Jean came back to the mountain, she remembered the rule about rocky paths. She saw two more paths. One path was muddy. One path was dusty. Tell Jean which path leads to the lake.

"Thank you," Jean said, and ran down the dusty path. Her striped legs were going very fast, and her striped hair was flying in the wind.

To be continued

Jean Makes the Red Stripes Disappear

Why did Jean have red stripes all over?

What could she do to make the red stripes disappear?

So which path was she taking?

Jean ran down the dusty path. Did the path lead to the mountain?

What's the rule about every dusty path?

Soon Jean came to the lake. But there were five little crumps on the path in front of her. Jean said, "I wonder if those little crumps are mean."

Tell Jean the rule about all little crumps.

The crumps began to run after Jean. Jean said, "Oh, my. Oh, dear. Oh, oh. I forgot what to say to make these mean crumps go away."

Tell Jean what to say.

Jean said, "Away, away." And what did the mean crumps do?

What's the rule about making mean

crumps go away?

After the mean crumps went away,
Jean jumped into the lake.⑤

Did the red stripes disappear?

What's the rule?

The red stripes disappeared, but now her
hair had turned white.

She said, "Oh, my. Oh, dear. I wish
the old wizard was here."

Suddenly, the wizard appeared. He said,
"Listen, my dear, and I will tell you the
rule for getting rid of your white hair. If
you stand on one foot, the white hair will
disappear."

Jean tried to say the rule five times.
But she couldn't do it. Help her out. Say
that rule for her.

At last, Jean said the rule. Then she
said, "But what and when . . . ."

The wizard disappeared.

To be continued

Jean Makes Her White Hair Go Away

Jean's hair had turned white. The wizard had told her what she had to do to make the white hair go away. What did she have to do?

Tell Jean the rule. See if you were right. Turn the page around and read the rule.

If you stand on one foot, the white hair will disappear.

Jean stood on one foot. Did her white hair go away?

Tell Jean the rule again.

Jean ran over to the lake. She bent down and looked at herself in the water. Then she said, "Oh, no." The white hair had gone away. But now Jean did not have any hair at all. She was bald. She felt the top of her head.

"Oh, no," she said. "I hate this place. I wish the wizard was here so that he could

215

tell me what to do." ⑤

Just then the wizard appeared. The wizard laughed when he looked at Jean. She said, "Don't laugh at me. I'm just trying to get out of this place."

The wizard said, "And you are doing a good job, my dear. You must know sixteen rules before you can leave the land of peevish pets. And look at all the rules you know. See if you can answer all of these questions."

Here are the questions the wizard asked:

1. What do you know about all little crumps?

2. How do you make mean crumps go away?

3. What do you know about every dusty path?

4. What do you know about every rocky path?

5. What do you know about red food?

6. What happens if you eat three red bananas?

7. How do you get rid of the red stripes?

8. How do you make white hair disappear?

The wizard said, "You already know eight rules."

Jean said, "I don't care. I want to know how to make my hair come back. I don't like to be bald."

The wizard said, "Here's the rule: If you want your hair back, clap your hands."

Help Jean say that rule.

More of this story next time

A Funny Animal Appears

The wizard told Jean a rule for getting her hair back. Tell Jean that rule.

Jean started to ask the wizard, "But what and when . . . ."

But the wizard disappeared before she could ask the question. Jean said, "I think I'll get my hair back." Jean clapped her hands. So did she get her hair back?

Jean felt her head. Her hair was back. She ran to the lake and looked at herself in the water. Her hair was back, but it was striped again.

She said, "Oh, well. I would rather have striped hair than be bald."

Just then a big, funny-looking animal came out of the lake. Part of that animal looked like a horse, and part of that animal looked like a monkey. The animal walked up to Jean and said, "I can help you get out of this place. I know all sixteen rules." ⑤

"Good," Jean said, "Teach me the rules I don't know."

The funny animal said, "Here's a good rule: All dusty paths lead to the mountain."

"No," Jean said. ★ "That's not right. Dusty paths do not lead to the mountain."

The animal looked very angry. He said, "Are you saying that I would tell a lie?"

"No," Jean said.

The talking animal said, "Here is another good rule: If you jump in the lake, you will get red stripes."

"No," Jean said. "If you jump in the lake, the stripes will disappear."

The talking animal looked very angry. "Do not say that I lie. Talking animals never lie. If you don't want to know the rules, I will not tell you any new rules."

Jean said, "Please tell me a new rule. I must know the rules so that I can leave this strange place."

"All right," the talking animal said.
"Here is a good rule: If you want to have
fun, say, 'Side, slide.'"

Help Jean say that rule.

"Thank you," Jean said. "I think I will
have some fun right now."

What can Jean say to have fun?

More next time

Jean Says, "Side, Slide."

What rule did the talking animal tell Jean?

Jean wanted to have some fun, so she said, "Side, slide." But she didn't have fun. All at once, she found herself up to her nose in snow. She was very cold. Snow was falling. The wind was howling. She shouted, "This is no fun. Wizard, where are you?"

The wizard popped out of a pile of snow. "Here I am," he said.

"Get me out of here," she shouted. "I'm cold. I want to be warm again."

Suddenly, the snow disappeared and Jean was warm again. She said, "What happened? I said, 'I want to be warm again,' and I was warm again."

The wizard smiled. He said, "That is the easiest rule in the land of peevish pets. If you want to be warm again, you say, 'I want to be warm again.'"⑤

Jean said the rule to herself five times.
Say it with her.

Then Jean sat down and said to the
wizard, "I don't understand something. That
talking animal told me a rule about having
fun. But the rule didn't work. He said, 'If
you want to have fun, say, "Side, slide."' But
I said those words, and I didn't have fun."

The old wizard laughed. Then he said,
"That talking animal told you the rule
for cold. Here's the rule: If you want to be
cold, say, 'Side, slide.'"

Jean said, "There are so many new
rules that I mix them up. Let's see if I
know the right rule. If you want to be cold,
say, 'Side, slide.'"

"That is right," the wizard said.

Jean said, "And if you want to be warm
again, you say, 'I want to be warm again.'"

"That is right," the wizard said.

Jean said both of those rules to herself

a few times. Then she said, "But why did that talking animal tell me a rule that didn't work? Doesn't he know the rules?"

"He knows them," the wizard said. "But there is a rule about talking animals. I'll ask you some questions. See if you can find out the rule."

The wizard asked, "Did that talking animal tell you the right rule about dusty paths?"

Then he asked, "Did he tell you the right rule about what would happen if you jumped in the lake?"

Then he asked, "Did he tell you the right rule about what would happen if you said, 'Side, slide'?"

Jean said, "I think I know the rule about talking animals."

More to come

Jean Figures Out a Rule

The talking animal had told Jean a rule about how to be cold. But he had told her that it was a rule for how to have fun.

What is the rule about how to be cold?

Then Jean had found out a rule for how to be warm again. Tell Jean that rule. If you don't remember it, turn the page around and read the rule.

If you want to be warm again, say, "I want to be warm again."

Now Jean was trying to figure out a rule about talking animals. She said to herself, "That talking animal lied to me when he told me the rule about the dusty path. He lied when he told me the rule about jumping in the lake. And he lied about what would happen if I said, 'Side, slide.' I think I know the rule about talking animals." ⑤

She turned to the wizard. "Here's the rule," she said. "Talking animals lie."

"That's right," the wizard said. "Never believe what a talking animal tells you. If he tells you that pink ice cream is good to eat, you know that pink ice cream is not good to eat. If he tells you that big crumps are very mean, you know that big crumps are not mean."

Jean said, "And if he tells you to eat three green apples, you know you shouldn't eat three green apples."

"That's right," the wizard said. "Now you know a rule about talking animals. Talking animals lie. Don't do what they tell you to do, or you will get in a mess."

"I will remember that," Jean said. "If a talking animal tells me to do something, I will not do it."

Jean ran her hand across her striped

hair. Then she began to ask the wizard a question. "But what and when . . . ." she said.

But the wizard had disappeared. Jean said to herself, "That's strange. Every time I say, 'But what and when . . . .' the wizard disappears."

Just then somebody said, "Hello." Jean looked around, but she did not see anybody.

"I am down here. I am a little bug." Jean bent down and looked at the bug. She said, "Are you a talking animal?"

"No," the bug said. "I never talk."

More next time

She Tricks a Talking Animal

Jean had met a talking bug. She said to herself, "This is a talking animal. There is a rule about talking animals, but I can't remember it." Tell Jean the rule about talking animals.

The bug said, "I will help you get out of here. I know all the rules, and I will tell you the best rules."

Jean had an idea about how to trick the talking animal. She said to herself, "If this animal says that something is fun, it won't be fun. If he tells me that something is good, it won't be good. If he tells me that something is bad, it won't be bad."

Jean smiled to herself. "I will ask him to tell me a rule about something that is really bad. But he won't tell me a rule about something that is bad. He will lie.⑤ He will tell me a rule about something that is good. I will trick him."

Jean said, "I have to find out more about the bad things in this place. Tell me a rule about something that is very, very bad."

The bug smiled and said, "Here's a rule about something that is really bad. If you tap your foot three times, you will turn into a snake."

"Thank you," Jean said. "You are a talking animal and I tricked you. I will tap my foot three times and see what happens."

"Don't do that," the bug cried. "You will be sad. You will be a snake. Don't do it."

Jean tapped her foot three times. Suddenly, she was flying like a bird. The wind was blowing her striped hair. She went down. Then she went up. "Wow," she said. Then she did a loop. "Wow," she said again. "This is more fun than anything."

She began to fly faster. Then she said, "I hope I remember the rule about flying."

What do you do if you want to fly? Tell Jean the rule.

Jean was flying over a town now. She looked down and saw a man that looked like the wizard. So she dropped down to the ground. But the man was not the wizard. He was very strange-looking. He stared at Jean and she stared at him. Then she said, "Hello, my name is Jean."

He said, "Bark, bark."

More to come

The Strange-Looking Man

What did Jean do so that she could fly?

What's the rule?

Who did she see when she was flying?

What did the strange-looking man say to her?

Jean said, "Can't you say anything but 'bark, bark'?"

The man said, "Squeak, squeak."

"I hate this place," Jean said. "I'm sorry that I ever wanted to dream about pets. I haven't seen a good pet in this place. I want to go home."

The man handed Jean a note. The note said, "This man is a pet. He is any kind of pet you want. He can be a cat, or a dog, or a horse, or a pig. Just tell him what kind of pet you want."

Jean looked at the man and said, "Let's see you be a dog." And the man became the word **dog**. The man became three letters, d-o-g.⑤

"This is too much," Jean said. She began to walk away. The letters d-o-g said, "Bark, bark."

"Oh, be quiet," Jean said. "Dogs don't say, 'Bark, bark.' They say, 'Woof, woof.'"

"Bark, bark," the letters said.

"I wish that old wizard was here," Jean said. "I want to find out more rules so I can get out of here."

Just then the wizard appeared. He said, "You have found out a rule about the man who can become letters."

"Yes," Jean said. "If you tell him to become a dog, he becomes the letters d-o-g."

"Very good," the wizard said. "Remember that rule, because I cannot tell you any more rules. You have to find out the last two rules by yourself."

Jean said, "But what and when . . . ."

The wizard disappeared.

She said, "Darn that wizard. Every time I say 'But what and when,' he disappears."

Suddenly, Jean jumped up. She said, "That's the rule for making the wizard disappear. If you want the wizard to disappear, you say, 'But what and when.'" Say that rule with Jean.

Jean needed only one more rule to leave the land of peevish pets.

This is almost the end.

Leaving the Land of Peevish Pets

Jean had found out fifteen rules. The last rule she found out told about making the wizard disappear. She needed only one more rule. So she sat down and began to think. Suddenly, she jumped up. She said, "I've got it. Every time I needed help, the wizard appeared. I think that's the rule. I'll find out." She stood up and yelled, "I need help."

Suddenly, the wizard appeared. Jean said, "I think I know all of the rules. I know how to make you appear. Here's the rule: If you want the wizard to appear, call for help."

"Good," the wizard said.

Then Jean said, "So now I can leave this land of peevish pets."

"That is right," the wizard said. "You have found out all the rules. So you may leave. Just close your eyes."

Jean closed her eyes. Suddenly, she felt something licking her face.⑤

She opened her eyes. She was in bed. Her mom and dad were standing near the bed, and there was a puppy on the bed. He ★ was licking Jean's face. He was black and brown and white. And he had a long tail. He was very pretty. Jean hugged him.

"Can I keep him?" she asked. "Can I, please?"

"He's your puppy," her mom said. Jean hugged the puppy harder. The puppy licked her face again.

Jean's mom said, "Somebody left this puppy for you. There was a note with him."

Jean's dad handed the note to Jean. The note said: "This dog is for Jean. His name is Wizard. And here is the rule about Wizard: If you love him and play with him, he will grow up to be the best dog in the land."

Jean was so happy that tears were running down her cheeks. She said, "Thank you, Wizard. Thank you very much."

She followed the rule, and her dog Wizard did become the very best dog in the land.

This is the end.